BEFORE YOU
STAT UP

How to
your star

G000059640

Pankaj Goyal

twitter @pango

 facebook https://www.facebook.com/BeforeYouStartUp

FP

FiNGERPRINT!

Reprint 2019

FiNGERPRINT!

An imprint of Prakash Books India Pvt. Ltd.

113/A, Darya Ganj, New Delhi-110 002,
Tel: (011) 2324 7062 – 65, Fax: (011) 2324 6975
Email: info@prakashbooks.com/sales@prakashbooks.com

facebook www.facebook.com/fingerprintpublishing
twitter www.twitter.com/FingerprintP
www.fingerprintpublishing.com

ISBN: 978 81 7599 440 9

Processed & printed in India

TO MY GRANDPARENTS:
Dadaji and Ammaji

ACKNOWLEDGEMENTS

I would have never written this book, but for my wife Swati. She convinced me to pen down my experiences as an entrepreneur. She also helped me structure and edit the book. I thank her for all this and for being in my life.

I thank all the entrepreneurs who spent the time and effort to share their journey with me. All of you are an inspiration to me!

Finally, thank you to Dipti from WordFamous, my literary guide; Shikha, my publisher; and Vidya, my editor for giving an opportunity to a first time author.

CONTENTS

BEFORE YOU
BUY THIS BOOK

I am not a successful entrepreneur. Else, you would have known me. You would have bought this book just by looking at the author's name. You would not be reading the first few pages as you are probably doing right now, contemplating whether the book is worth buying.

Then, who am I to give you advice about starting up and why should you buy this book?

I will answer this question first. If you are convinced, proceed to reading the rest of this book. If not, do not waste your time and money. Keep the book back on the shelf or just close your browser window.

My story

I am an ex-entrepreneur. I started a company in 2008 and quit after three years. I shut down the company. In diplomatic words, I was not-so-successful as an entrepreneur. In honest words, I failed.

I believe I had all the ingredients to succeed. Born into a middle class family in a tier-2 city (Jaipur), I had the hunger to be successful, rich, and famous. I had been preparing for it since my school days, following the "standard path" and succeeding at each step. I went to the best schools (IIT Kanpur and IIM Bangalore), got excellent grades, and got the perfect job in a top tier management consulting firm (McKinsey & Company). I underwent training on running a business. I worked hard, put in long hours, and gave it my absolute best. I chased my dream relentlessly.

However, I did not succeed in my venture.

I had an excellent start. Year one was fantastic. We built the product prototype in two months, got our first customer in nine months, grew to about fifty thousand customers, and became cash positive in fifteen months.

And then it all stagnated and went downhill.

In Year two, we failed to scale up the product. Sales stagnated. I failed to build my team. No new products. No pivot. No growth. I had differences with my co-founder on the future of the company. I could not fix these issues. After battling for over a year, I decided to quit.

So, where did I go wrong? Was it in Year two?

On the surface, yes. But on further reflection I realised that the real mistakes happened before I even started up. I messed up the preparation before starting up. The chaos in year two was the result of poor preparation before day One. There was no way to build a strong building over a shaky foundation.

Why I decided to write this book?

"Bhaiya, I'm bored of my job. I am capable of so much more! I also want to launch a startup!"

I was catching up with my young neighbour, casually sipping a cup of hot tea on a foggy morning in February 2011. I was getting married the next day. There was a lot on my mind. The last thing I wanted to talk about was startups and the startup life, having already answered a million questions on my business from curious relatives and friends over the past week.

From what I remembered, the twenty-three-year-old eager adult standing in front of me had been a sincere student throughout school and had managed to get into a tier-1 engineering college through hard work. He was good at coding and had seemed pleased to land a steady job with a reputed software company in Bangalore. I was meeting him for the first time since he had started earning. I could see changes in his standard of living—he was using the latest iPhone and had an expensive watch. He had learnt to spend on himself, which is a difficult skill to pick up for middle class kids in India. I was happy for him—that he was financially independent and ready to build his career.

"So, what do you think?" He was anxiously waiting for an enthusiastic embrace and a high-five with a punch in the air.

"Are you sure? Do you even know what it means? Have you prepared well for it?" I responded with sincerity and good intentions.

His reaction was a mix of shock and anger. He had assumed I would support his decision and expected a warm welcome from a current entrepreneur. Instead, he felt belittled at my unexpected response.

"What do you mean I don't know? What do you mean by preparation? I can start tomorrow if I want . . ."

He is not the only one who has approached me with an intention to start up. Several people in my network—friends, family, colleagues, batchmates—most of them in their twenties, highly qualified and capable, and some of them in well-paying jobs—have approached me with similar questions over the years. "I want to start up. I have an idea. How should I go about it?" And each time my answer has been, "Are you sure? Do you even know what it means? How are you preparing for it?"

Eric Reiss, the author of the pioneering book *"The Lean Startup"* writes:

"When we fail, as so many of us do, we have a ready-made excuse: We did not have the right stuff. We were not visionary enough or were not in the right place at the right time. After more than ten years as an entrepreneur, I came to reject that line of thinking. . . .Startup success is not a consequence of good genes or being in the right place at the right time. Startup success can be engineered by following the right process, which means it can be learned, which means it can be taught." (Reiss, 2011).

In my three years as an entrepreneur, I believe I have been through the whole gamut of experiences that characterise a startup journey—from euphoria to realism, from happiness to despair, and from success to failure. Since then, I have reflected what I could have done differently as an entrepreneur and what the "right process" should look like to achieve a different outcome. I spoke to several other entrepreneurs in my network from diverse backgrounds, industries, and sectors, who are at different stages of their journey, to compare notes and gain additional perspective.

Finally, I decided to compile my learnings, so that you, the reader, do not have to reinvent the wheel.

What this book will focus on?

This book focuses on a critical, but often overlooked part of an entrepreneur's journey, i.e. preparation before starting up.

Let's look at a typical startup journey:

Pre-day One: All that you do before you enter the battlefield.

Day One: You start

Year one: You try to figure it out. Peaks and troughs, rollercoaster ride.

Year two: Your business model matures. You find a better product/market fit.

Year three and beyond: Your company grows exponentially or stagnates, or collapses. You know the future of your company by year three.

Figure 1: Phases of The Startup Journey

You might notice from this chart that once you start up, there is a lot of uncertainty. Your control over your own fate and future diminishes. External forces—customers, investors, employees, regulators, and more—take over.

However, you are in much more control until day one. That's where I will focus on.

Your own preparation is the only thing you can completely control.

Preparing to start up involves having a better understanding of the forces that can kill your business and having a strategy to win against them. It also means gaining a better understanding of yourself—what motivates you, how you deal with your family, your career, your finances, and how to manage stress.

To quote from the legendary Silicon Valley investor Peter Thiel's book *Zero to One*, "*Thiel's law: a startup messed up at its foundation cannot be fixed*" (Thiel, 2014).

My aim with this book is to help you lay down a strong foundation for your venture through solid preparation before starting up.

I am not going to talk about year two and year three in this book. In fact, I will not even talk about how to build products, how to raise funds or how to scale up. There is plenty of authoritative literature available on these topics.

Finally, I do not intend to prescribe a specific step-by-step process to start up. Each startup is unique. Like each human being, each startup follows a different path of growing up, learning, maturing, and dying.

Reid Hoffman, the co-founder of LinkedIn, said about

startups, "You jump off a cliff and you assemble an airplane on the way down".

This book is intended to help you prepare for that jump. It can help you learn what are the different parts of the plane, how much time it will take for you to touch the ground, what the cloud conditions are, which tools you will need, how to switch paths, how to keep your cool, and offer answers to many more questions like these. The actual jump and the actual assembly will still be unique, and you may encounter new situations or information as you fall. If you prepare well, your chances of success should increase.

Why preparation is important?

Statistics reveal that anywhere between 70% and 90% businesses fail within the first two to three years. The odds are against you to succeed.

Why is it so risky to start a new business?

Here's an explanation: each business is exposed to multiple external forces. Customer preferences, competition, capital, internal team dynamics, law of the land, your mind itself—to name a few. These forces are strong, unpredictable, and most of the times, beyond your control. Even if one of these forces hits you hard, your business is dead. Your entrepreneurship journey is a battle against these forces.

Let me give you an example.

You want to set up a social media consulting service which helps small and medium businesses to acquire customers through social channels (Facebook, YouTube, Twitter, WhatsApp etc.). Your business can fail if any of the following happen:

- Your potential client—a small business owner—does not understand the power of social media; is not interested in learning about it; is definitely not interested in paying to learn about it.
- Your potential client turns out to be savvy with social media; does not need your advice or expertise; believes it can be done without your help.
- Your potential client has not used social media in the past; is excited and willing to pay you, but target customer base is not on social media. Your services are of no help.
- Social media channels start providing similar services. You are doomed.
- Your team breaks apart. The best team member realises she can set up her own consulting firm.
- You lose interest after six months and quit.

And many more such situations . . .

So, what can you do about these forces? First step is to be aware. Second step is to prepare. More you know, better you can prepare to fight. Research has proven that the better you prepare, the higher are your chances of survival and success in entrepreneurship.

Adam Grant is a renowned author and professor of psychology at Wharton University. In his recent book, "*Originals*," where he tries to understand common patterns among original thinkers in our society, he writes, ". . .the most successful ones [entrepreneurs] are not the daredevils who leap before they look. They are the ones who reluctantly tiptoe to the edge of the cliff, calculate the rate of descent, triple-check their parachutes, and set up a safety net at the bottom just in case." (Grant, 2017).

Professor William Sahlman of Harvard Business School echoes the same thought, "One of the great myths about entrepreneurs is that they are risk seekers. All sane people want to avoid risk."

My conversations with entrepreneurs confirm this finding. Almost every one of them had done their homework before starting up. Their secret? They managed their risks by preparing well.

Despite being so important, preparation is often overlooked and ignored. Aspiring entrepreneurs either have no clue about this phase or do not know how to prepare. In fact, "Just do it," "Jump in blind," "it is an adventure" are all glamorised folktales. Biographers or autobiographers of entrepreneurs usually gloss over "pre-startup" days completely. What a perfect recipe for disaster!

You prepare for your cricket match, for your examinations, for your hiking trip, for your love proposal, even for your food—why make an exception when it comes to chasing the biggest dream of your life?

One of my favourite examples that can be related to a successful startup is that of two of our very own legendary cricketers.

In the never-ending debate of "Sachin Tendulkar vs. Rahul Dravid (two cricket legends): Who is better?" my vote has always been for Dravid.

I don't care about what they did: how many runs they scored, or how many matches they won. Both are legends. But I cannot imagine myself ever aspiring to be a Sachin. But I can imagine myself aspiring to be a Dravid.

Let me explain why?

Sachin was gifted, a genius. He worked hard to convert his genius into long-lasting success. There is a lot to learn from his dedication and focus.

But Dravid was a workhorse. He prepared. He worked hard. He analysed. He knew his strengths and weaknesses like no one else. When he was batting, he was in a "zen-like" mode, in his "zone." When he was off the field, he was completely at peace with who he was, why he was criticised, and why the team needed him. The world's fastest bowler at one point, Shoaib Akhtar from Pakistan feared Dravid, not Sachin. He said, "Dravid would bore you, he would tire you out. He is like Muhammad Ali, he would tire you out and then knock you out."

I am not a genius. In fact, most of us are not. We cannot plan and prepare to be a genius. But I can imagine preparing and working hard to become a Dravid in my chosen field.

The goal of this book is to encourage you to become a "Dravid" of entrepreneurship. To help you prepare yourself so well that you can fight any pitch condition, any bowler, any sledging, and any crowd.

Who should read this book?

You should read this book if you are a . . .

"Wannabe" entrepreneur in school or college

Are you a starry-eyed high school or college kid, who idolises Mark Zuckerberg or Steve Jobs or Elon Musk or Bill Gates or a successful entrepreneur from your college? Have you memorised the names of founders of all the hot startups in India

and the Silicon Valley? Do you regularly read TechCrunch and
YourStory, and attend all the talks by a VC or an entrepreneur?
Do you plan on participating in all the possible business plan
competitions and dream about "the dropout who ruled the
world" stories? Do you plan to start up someday?

This book is for you. It can take you from your fantasy
dream world to reality. It can help you be realistic and prepare
better.

"Friday-night-after-two-drinks" reluctant entrepreneur in your 20s/30s

Are you two years into your first job, someone who finds it
boring and hates your boss? Do you plan to do an MBA but are
too lazy to prepare? Are you someone who has no big mortgages
and no family responsibilities and knows one person who left
your company and became an entrepreneur? Do you want to
start up to reset your career, or because you always wanted to
be an entrepreneur? Do you have a new business plan every
month, but nothing happens, ever?

Or maybe you are in your thirties with more than ten years
of professional life with good savings, a house, and car(s); you
have family responsibilities; you are facing the mid-life crisis
and looking for a new adventure in life; you are thinking about
a startup as a channel to break the monotony of life.

This book is for you.

It can help you decide whether a startup is your destiny
and help you systematically plan to start up within a timeframe
instead of just dream about it.

"Ready to go" soon-to-be entrepreneur

Are you someone who has finalised a business plan and done some basic homework? Are you raring to go and start a company?

This book is for you.

It can help you assess whether you are ready to go or not, identify the gaps, and learn how to fill these gaps.

"Already on the train, but less than 12 months" entrepreneur

Are you someone who started up recently? Have you gone through one or two cycles of ups and downs? Are you stabilising further or struggling more?

This book is for you.

It can help you understand the issues, pinpoint the most important ones, and solve them.

Loved ones of any of the above (boyfriend, girlfriend, parents, etc.)

Are you the loved one of any of the above? Have you no idea exactly what is going through your mind? Are you concerned out of ignorance or with reason?

This book is for you.

It can help you understand the daily life of entrepreneurs, the situations they face, and how you can support (or stop) them.

A real/aspiring VC/angel investor who has never built a business

Are you an aspiring or current VC/investor, who has never started anything? Are you someone who can paint the big macro picture, but does not know how to start a business and run it? Are you an expert at making "observations" on startup pitches but do not how to evaluate them properly?

This book is for you.

It can help you get into the mind of an entrepreneur, empathise with them, and make better judgement calls.

In Closing

I am not a star entrepreneur trying to sell my story. I am not a VC telling you to "think big and change the world" so he can have that one blockbuster to compensate for his ninety-nine failed ventures. I am not trying to be the new "visionary" thinker.

I am just one of you. I have been "you" at some point in my life. I understand your dreams, your ambitions, your anxieties, and your fears and I want to help you by sharing my experiences and those of others in my network, along with the life-lessons I have learned.

I will tell you the truth like it is. I will show you the reality behind starting up. I will bust many myths. You might not like the truth and that's OKAY. I am not here to massage your ego. I will tell you if a startup is NOT for you. I am here to help you ask the right questions and make the right decisions.

I believe failure teaches you far more than success does. Failure is not easy. It hurts. It is one of life's harshest teachers.

And the one thing I have learnt is this: what NOT to do is as important as knowing what to do. <u>This book can help you because it will tell you what NOT to do.</u> Most success stories will not tell you this.

You will also gain insights about the psychological aspects of running a startup: you might have the best idea in the world, but you need a healthy mind to follow through on it. There is no dearth of advice on ideas, business cases, product development, marketing, customer acquisition cost, and other aspects of running a startup, but seldom do we discuss the mind of the entrepreneur.

This book might come out as biased towards "internet entrepreneurship," or "online entrepreneurship." I do not blame you if you think so. Most of the people I talked to, and the examples I will draw, belong to this domain of entrepreneurship. However, these principles are valid regardless of the type of entrepreneurship. Whether you are planning to set up a manufacturing unit, or a fast food franchise, or a brick and mortar retail store—the preparation is similar. The questions are still the same—the absolute answer will vary by industry or type of business, or size of company.

My intention is not to discourage you by showing the dark side of entrepreneurship. On the contrary, my goal is to make you aware of this dark side and help you prepare a strong foundation to succeed.

Okay! Over to you. If what I have said so far piques your interest, read on. I hope you enjoy this book!

Still not convinced? No problem! Thank you for your time. Connect with me @pango on Twitter if you would like to chat!

CHAPTER ONE

So You Want to Be an Entrepreneur. Think again

"STARTING UP IS MY DREAM"

I wanted to be a rich and famous entrepreneur. But nobody told me how hard it was going to be.

Ever since I was in high school, I wanted to be an entrepreneur. I was inspired by Bill Gates and Steve Jobs and what they had accomplished with Microsoft and Apple, respectively. I wanted to be just like them—a rich, famous, and successful owner of a big technology company. This desire continued to grow in college and business school, where I attended talks by famous venture capitalists and successful Indian entrepreneurs, and listened to each one of them extolling the virtues of entrepreneurship. I was starstruck.

In hindsight, I was being naïve. None of the success stories I read or heard about mentioned how hard it would be to start a new business and survive, let alone be successful at it. Nobody explained the hard realities behind the glamour and money. Nobody mentioned that for every one success story in the news, there were nine failed ones that nobody talked about.

It was like someone wanting to climb Mt. Everest after seeing a picture of it in a geography book and reading about Edmund Hillary and Tenzing Norgay successfully scaling the peak.

Having ambition is certainly not wrong. In fact, it is a prerequisite for being successful. But ambition alone is not enough. It needs to be supplemented with a healthy dose of reality. And the reality is as follows.

There is a 90% chance that you will fail.

Accept this fact and work with it.

So, what makes entrepreneurship such a risky proposition?

CB Insights, an analyst firm, did an extensive survey talking to founders from more than 150 companies that had failed in their mission and were shut down. They wanted to understand why these startups failed. The sample set of startups is fairly well-represented, ranging from well-funded and unfunded, hyped about and unknown, experienced and inexperienced founding team, and a variety of businesses from music streaming to food delivery, though there is a bias towards internet businesses.

The research zeroed in on twenty of the most common reasons why startups fail. You can read the full report online (CBS Insights. "The 20 Reasons Startups Fail." https://www.cbinsights.com/research/startup-failure-reasons-top/). I am synthesising the findings to five major themes:

1. Your product is the problem
2. Your competition kills you
3. The legal system kills you

4. You run out of cash
5. Your team is weak

1. Your product is the problem

Have you heard of Segway? It is a personal two-wheel self-balancing scooter. Segway was built to revolutionise urban transport. Back in 2001, Segway was at the peak of its hype. Prominent Venture Capitalists (VCs) poured money into the idea. P.C. Kamen, the creator of the Segway, unveiled it as the "human transporter," claiming that it "will be to the car what the car was to the horse and buggy."

Segway turned out to be a big flop. It was too fast for sidewalks and too slow for roadways. There was no space for storage. It ended up as a niche device used for tourism purposes. You can find a Segway tour in most big tourist attractions around the world.

Segway is a clear example of the single most important reason why startups fail: Building an offering with no real value to the target customer.

Often, the problem is real for a small set of customers, but irrelevant for a broader customer base.

I helped two friends build UniversityHiring, a web-based portal to automate and manage the recruitment process for college placement offices. IIM Bangalore had a complex placement process and was one of our first customers. However, as we talked to tier-2 and tier-3 colleges to market and sell our automation tool, we found few takers. Apart from a handful of top tier engineering and management colleges that had companies lining up at their doors, most colleges wanted help in finding jobs for their students. Placement officers cared more about getting more companies to come to their campuses, rather than simplifying the process. Our product was just not relevant to our larger customer base.

Akshat Choudhary, a serial entrepreneur, and founder of BlogVault (a backup service for WordPress) and ActivMob (an SMS-based group messaging service), talks about his early days in the workforce (Choudhary A., 2016):

"I had just joined Citrix, receiving a salary for the first time. I was prudent with my money. But I was spending without tracking my expenses. So, I built an app to track my expenses over SMS."

The expense-tracking app did not do well in the marketplace. While Akshat had built a good product that served his own needs, his Gen Y target customer base was not as careful about their spending habits and did not seem to want it.

Sometimes a solution requires a major behaviour change from customers. Influencing behaviour is difficult, even if the benefit is substantial and real.

Take the example of fitness devices or healthy diets, or even going to the gym. Do people understand the benefits of a healthy lifestyle? Yes, of course they do. But how many do it? Not many. Because it means changing or influencing behaviour.

Sangeet Paul Choudhary, founder of Platformation Labs, is an international best-selling author, chair of the MIT Platform Summit, and an appointed member of the World Economic Forum's Global Future Council.

Sangeet's venture is in the business of ideas and intellectual capital, where the currency of success is, in addition to revenues, global influence.

According to him, productisation of intellectual capital comes with inherent risks:

"First, your idea might not be good enough.

Second, assuming it is good, it might not reach your desired audience. For instance, it might be easy to come up with a body of work but very difficult to have it adopted by Fortune 100 CEOs and world leaders.

Third, assuming it is good and accepted by people, it still does not mean you can achieve your goals (of money or influence or others)."

There is no defined business model or template that can be followed here. You cannot say: If I do x, y, and z, I can build a company. There are not many others who have built global influence from scratch!

Have you seen other examples of products which have missed the customer? Have you rejected business ideas which sounded cool to you, but had a limited customer demand? Talk to me at @pango on Twitter.

2. Your competition kills you

No idea is unique. Once you are in the market, you will find some company fighting against you.

What if your competitors' **product is better** than yours—in terms of features and/or cost?

Have you heard of Mint.com? It is a personal finance product, which was acquired by Intuit for $170 million. Around the same time, another startup, Wesabe was working on a very similar idea. It was a close second player for a long time. While Mint was successful, Wesabe closed down within a few years. Even though market demand existed, one company succeeded and the other failed. The reason was the difference in user experience—how the two companies enabled customers to use their service in a complex interaction. Mint understood customer requirements better and offered a better user experience (http://blog.precipice.org/why-wesabe-lost-to-mint/).

Facebook won against Myspace and Orkut. The reason: It was a superior product.

What if your competitor has access to more resources (cash, people, brand, IP, access to customers, etc.)?

Sidecar was an on-demand car service. It started as a car sharing service and moved to on-demand delivery services. It competed well against the bigger rivals: Uber and Lyft. But beyond a point, the company was just out-funded. Sidecar CEO Sunil Paul noted, "Sidecar had a 'significant capital disadvantage.' Lyft has raised \$1.26 billion and Uber has raised over \$10 billion. Sidecar has only raised \$35 million. It was impossible to compete in this space." ("Sidecar is calling it quits on rides and deliveries." December 29, 2015. https://techcrunch.com/2015/12/29/sidecar-is-calling-it-quits-on-rides-and-deliveries/).

Kato was a startup built to offer a business focused chat app. It failed to get significant traction to fight against its formidable rival, Slack. As its CEO and Co-founder Andrei Soroker wrote in the obituary email, "Slack ate the world." ("Chat App Kato will shut down." August 13, 2015. http://venturebeat.com/2015/07/13/chat-app-kato-will-shut-down-on-aug-31-because-slack/).

3. The legal system kills you

You might hit the dreadful scenario when your product is found non-compliant with the law of the land.

HomeJoy was an online platform to connect customers with home service providers, including house cleaners and handymen—it was essentially the "Uber" of house cleaning services. It hit a snag when it faced four lawsuits over whether its employees should be classified as employees or contractors. The lawsuits made fund raising difficult and ultimately the company had to shut down. ("Cleaning services startup Homejoy shuts down." 2015. http://www.recode.net/2015/7/17/11614814/ cleaning-services-startup-homejoy-shuts-down-after-battling-worker).

Ordrx was a New York-based restaurant technology company. It achieved early success with $1.4 million venture capital from Google Ventures and 500 startups, and had 20 employees. Things were going well, until they were hit by patent lawsuits, which forced them into court. With high legal fees, it was impossible for the company to survive for long. (Bloom, David, Co-founder of Ordrx. "Why this Google-backed *Brooklynite* says Congress could have saved his business." August 10, 2015. http://www.bizjournals.com/newyork/news/2015/08/10/ david-bloom-ordrx-google-ventures-patent-troll.html)

If your company hits a legal battle, it is an ominous situation. The legal proceedings and fees can suck the life out of your team and bank balance. Sometimes, as in the case of Ordrx, you have no other choice but to shut down the business.

4. You run out of cash

Cash is the fuel that keeps a business running. Cash is your best friend and your deadliest enemy. If the business runs out of cash, it is as good as dead.

Imagine a situation where you have a prototype ready and it is working well. You are all set to move forward, but you have no money left to spend on product development. Uh-oh.

PatterBuzz (http://patterbuzz.com/2015/03/down-but-not-out/) was founded as a way to consume premium content over the Internet. The founder was proud of the way things were going after its launch. The company had content licenses with 50+ magazines and had published 450+ issues and 20,000+ articles. PatterBuzz seemed to be on the path towards decent success, until it had no money left to fund operations. The founder tried to raise funds but could not, due to multiple reasons. Finally, he ran out of cash and had to shut shop.

Wardrobe Wake-up (http://www.bizjournals.com/boston/blog/startups/2015/03/funding-woes-cause-subscription-based-fashion.html) matched customers with stylists. It was a subscription service that started well with a waitlist of around 1,500 customers. But the founders could not secure funding and were forced to down the shutters.

What if you run into a situation where you have a product ready, your initial set of customers are onboard, you are ready to scale up by launching your first big marketing campaign or buying new servers; but you run out of cash? What a bummer!

After the expense tracking app did not find traction in the market, Akshat Choudhary (BlogVault and ActivMob) realised that people were more interested in an SMS-based group chat product. So, he pivoted and launched ActivMob. The product was a hit, with the user base growing at a good clip and the product receiving good media. However, it was capital intensive due to high SMS delivery costs. Akshat tried to raise money, but he could not. Finally, he had no option but to close down.

One of the fundamental issues in a startup is typically the absence of a growth model with which the company can acquire new customers in a profitable and sustainable way. If the company has to spend cash to acquire each new customer, and the acquired customer is not profitable quickly enough, the company's cash will deplete very quickly, ultimately leading to its demise.

Several startups in the e-commerce and food delivery sectors in India have closed down due to their capital intensive nature and the lack of deep pockets required to acquire and sustain customers.

5. Your team is weak

People are the biggest asset of any startup. Quite often, startups fail because:

- The startup team might not have the required level of expertise and skill sets required to create a quality offering
- The startup team might not have the required level of experience to run the business, or
- The startup team might not have the killer attitude to execute with speed and precision.

Sometimes, a member of the founding team itself might be the weak link.

What if your technology co-founder turns out to be a dud? You can see that product development is not moving fast enough and quality is poor.

And what if the CEO of your startup fails miserably in her or his duties, with no experience in running a business of that size in the past?

Sometimes, the founder(s) cannot find the right people to run or grow the business.

Consider a scenario where your head of sales is not a rock star. You hired her because she was the only one affordable and willing to join a startup. Now, she is a liability.

Whatever might be lacking, a weak team will die, and starting a company with such a team can quickly turn into a losing battle against competition and the market.

It is a tough pill to swallow and something that takes some time to figure out—but unfortunately startups just do not have the luxury of time. Many times, it is too late before founders recognise and accept their own weaknesses or their teams' shortcomings.

The market is not the only enemy; you will face multiple personal challenges.

We saw how market forces are your enemies when you startup—but they are not the only ones. Your own expectations of what your life should look like will be different from what might happen.

1. Your bank balance will make you cringe
2. Your lifestyle will go for a toss
3. Your personal and social commitments will take a backseat
4. You will always be stressed, in some cases depressed
5. Your family will worry. Sharmaji's son will continue to torture you.
6. Your career will take a hit

Let's take a look at how each of these can wreak havoc on your personal life.

1. Your bank balance will make you cringe

Let's talk about two friends: Arun and Raj. Both are ambitious and work hard to get into a top tier business school. Both study hard and get good grades.

Raj lands a job in a top investment bank in New York. He joins the bank with a hefty new-hire bonus. He rents an apartment close to Times Square. He enjoys expensive dinners. He often travels to exotic destinations on long weekends and vacations.

Arun lands a similar offer from a rival bank, but his heart is set on starting his own startup venture—and he decides to reject the bank's offer. Arun moves to Bangalore. He rents a small apartment in an inexpensive area. He focuses his energy on building his product. He works long hours. He tries to save as much as possible. He denies himself most meals out. He travels cheaply, and only when absolutely necessary for his business.

Assuming both start with a bank balance of INR 1,00,000 each at the beginning of the year, here is what the situation might look like at the end of year one:

End of year one	
Raj	INR 30,00,000
Arun	INR 30,000

(Remember, Arun has no income; only expenses this year)

Raj continues his dream run in New York and moves into year two with the job. The economy is doing well. He hits a jackpot with a big bonus. The cash registers keep ringing for him.

Arun launches his product after six months. His product receives rave reviews and he receives some initial funding from angel investors. He has ten customers so far, but only one pays. He decides to withdraw a salary of INR 6 lacs a year.

End of year two	
Raj	INR 1,00,00,000
Arun	INR 3,00,000

Raj is promoted at the end of year two. He thinks of buying an apartment in New York, getting married, and settling down.

Arun's business is not taking off as expected. He is making some changes to his product. He is hoping for exponential growth once the new version is released. He has expanded his team. But his salary is still the same.

End of year three	
Raj	INR 2,50,00,000
Arun	INR 5,00,000

Raj ends up with a bank balance that is fifty times Arun's after the first three years. This gap only widens with time.

You could be Arun. Your best friend in college could be Raj.

How would you feel about earning significantly less than your friends and peers? How would you feel if you had no idea when this disparity will end?

How would you feel if your friends posted pictures of their new Porsche or their latest five-star business-class travel? Would you cringe and think "What the hell. That could have been me!"

How would you feel if your employees earned more than you? You know you have to retain them. As a founder, you will be the last one to be paid—after your employees, suppliers, investors—that is, if anything is left at the end.

How would you feel if you did not have the freedom to increase your own salary? You would need your investors' permission. Or you might want to re-invest excess cash into the business.

How would you feel if you personally ran into a cash crunch situation like say, the risk of defaulting on your car loan or your mortgage?

Here is the reality.

A monthly paycheck is good. A monthly paycheck is real.

Living without a consistent monthly paycheck is tough. And when your peers earn more, it gets tougher.

Equity is awesome. Startup glamour and prestige is great.

However, the truth is: cash is real and cash rules.

2. Your lifestyle will go for a toss

As we saw in the case of Arun, when you do not have a regular monthly paycheck, you might have to start making small sacrifices in your day-to-day personal life. These small trade-offs start to feel bigger over time.

My consulting job had spoilt me. Five-star hotel stays, dinners, business-class travel, a free phone, free internet, etc. I was living the good life.

Then one day, I quit my job and boarded a flight to Delhi to start up. The moment I landed, my lifestyle changed. Overnight.

All the perks I had enjoyed in my job vanished. No more luxury living. I had just entered the "startup entrepreneur" mode.

I stayed in a modest apartment in Dwarka. Luckily, it was almost winter and so, I didn't need air-conditioning straight away. I used the Delhi Metro to commute. It was the most convenient form of transport. The realities of life hit me hard when I had to travel to Mumbai on business. Suddenly, I had to make serious choices. Plane or train? Home food or eat out? Should I spend on new clothes? Party or not? These small lifestyle choices and sacrifices started to pile up.

How would you feel if:

- train vs. flight, taxi vs. metro, etc. became real choices?
- you had to cut down on your monthly entertainment budget?
- you had to cut down on eating out?
- you had to downgrade your car or even your home?

If you are looking for a lifestyle career, a startup is not the right choice!

3. Your personal and social commitments will take a backseat

On top of all that I described so far, you will have to work harder. Running a startup is a 24/7 job. No weekends, no "time-offs".

How would you feel if you:

- had to compromise on your fitness and exercise schedule?
- had to work on weekends?
- had to compromise on spending time with your family?
- cannot find the time to meet your friends? And eventually, they stopped caring?
- could not find time to date or meet new people?

How would you feel about making these personal sacrifices?

4. You will always be stressed and in some cases depressed

The loss of control over your future that starting up brings can result in stress and anxiety.

Siddhartha Agrawal, Founder of Wallsoft Labs, a high frequency trading firm (Agrawal, 2016), had a good start to his venture. He had an anchor client, so he was generating cash from month One. Not many entrepreneurs have this luxury. Yet, he felt the stress. He felt the pain of pushing himself.

"The uncertainties can be very stressful, as one is continuously trying to build on the strengths while covering the weaknesses."

Pause for a moment and think: how would you feel if you could not make long-term personal commitments (like marriage or having a baby) because you have no idea how your future will shape up?

How would you feel if you could not sleep properly due to all the stress? Founders are said to sleep like babies—waking up crying every few hours!

Chaya Jadhav is a serial entrepreneur. She was the co-founder and CEO of VirtualMob—an augmented reality B2B SaaS Platform out of London, which was acquired in 2014. Her current role is advising startups on growth and product strategy (Jadhav, 2016).

Chaya remembers her tough days.

"The toughest part for me as an entrepreneur was during the boot strap phase, when we didn't have much runway left (6 months) and we had to get the product out and prove traction to the investors. I hardly slept at nights!"

Starting a business is a psychological game. Your mind can play tricks on you. The experience can shock you. You may "turn into" someone you do not recognise. Emotions may surge up and dominate you—feelings that you were never aware existed in you. You may have dark thoughts about yourself—doubting your real talents or skills or abilities. You may doubt your original strength of will. You may become critical for the first time of friends and loved ones who may not seem supportive anymore. You may sink into a "What is the use, anyway?" sort of apathy. In extreme cases, you might face mental depression.

Mohan Rajagopalan, Founder of Yaap.io, a big data analytics platform based out of the Silicon Valley, shares his perspective. (Rajagopalan, 2016).

"You read a lot of inspirational stuff---the popular stuff that sells. In reality, it is a lot of hard work, very tough choices that makes you aware of who you are as a human being. It is also very lonely, because it makes you realise who your friends are and who will stick by you as sources of support. And you do need every ounce of support you can get."

How would you feel about the uncertainties that entrepreneurship presents?

5. Your family will worry. Sharmaji's son will continue to torture you

It would be unfair to say that the Indian society does not support entrepreneurship. We have millions of small entrepreneurs. Many social groups are known for their entrepreneurial spirit. The concept of "jugaad" follows the principle of maximizing output with constrained resources—which aligns well with the underlying spirit of entrepreneurship.

Then where is the gap?

Indian society does not like risk-taking.

Parents who have been businessmen or businesswomen might be delighted, and very supportive if their child starts a business (though even they might prefer a known industry). In fact, the same parents might become nervous if their child wants to pursue higher education—there is always a fear of the unknown!

Siddhartha Agrawal, (Wallsoft Labs), got lucky.

"Convincing my family was not very difficult because some

of the previous generations in my family had been entrepreneurs, and I was still young enough to experiment, fail, and get a job again if needed."

On the other hand, people who have worked in a stable "job" throughout their career might freak out if their child or loved one wants to start a new business. And if your parents or relatives fall in that category, you may have a tough time convincing them!

Do you remember the world's most successful man, "Sharma ji ka beta"? He haunted you in your school, college, job, and even your personal life. Once you decide to start up, he will be back, with a vengeance!

Let's take a look at what an entrepreneur son's conversation with his concerned mother would sound like.

Mom: Beta, kya chal raha hai aaj kal?
Me: Sab theek hai mummy, kaam me busy rehta hoon.
Mom: Beta, ye business vagerah ke chakkar me kyun pad gaye ho tum. Acchi khaasi job chhod di. Bagalwale Sharmaji ke bete ko dekho—London me job kar raha hai, naya flat bhi khareeda hai.
Me: Ichcha thi bas khud kuch karne ki, aap chinta mat karo
Mom: Aaj kal ke bachche sunte kahan hain! Abhi shaadi bhi nahi hui hai. Pata nahi kaun karega isse shaadi! Sharmaji ka beta to honeymoon ke liye New Zealand bhi ho aaya.
Me: Hmm
Mom: Achcha apna dhyaan rakhna. Paison ki zaroorat ho to bata dena
Me: Ji mummy

(**Mom**: Son, what are you up to these days?

Me: Everything is okay mummy, I just stay busy with work

Mom: Son, what have you gotten yourself into? Left a decent job. Look at our neighbour Sharmaji's son—he is working in London and has recently bought a new apartment.

Me: I just wanted to do something on my own, don't worry

Mom: Kids these days don't even listen! He is not even married yet---who will want to marry him! Sharmaji's son just came back from a honeymoon in New Zealand!

Me: Hmm

Mom: Okay take care of yourself. Let me know if you need money

Me: Yes mummy)

Visualise how you would feel when phone conversations with your mom became increasingly painful for you?

How would you feel when you have to start avoiding talking to or meeting your family members, because you have no satisfactory answers to their questions?

Even if you hide yourself in the remotest corner of the world, questions from our society will come to haunt you. Your favourite Sharmaji's son will never leave you alone.

6. Your career will take a hit

Say you fail or quit after spending a couple of years trying to build a startup. How will the market look at you and your startup experience? Can you restart at a level higher in someone else's company? Can you return to the big corporate environment you left a couple of years ago?

How will you feel if the market discounts your time spent on your startup?

You took the risk, worked 24/7, and learned ten times more than you would in a normal job. How will you feel if the market completely ignored your hard work and learnings?

How will you feel if the market penalises you for your failure? How will you feel if the startup failure becomes a permanent blot on your CV?

How will you feel when you realiseyou might have essentially lost the years spent on building on your startup?

My dear Reader—there is no rational reason to become an entrepreneur. Entrepreneurship is a struggle. Often, a painful one.

Ben Horowitz, in his book *"The Hard Thing about Hard Things"* describes this struggle very well. I am quoting him verbatim below (Horowitz, 2014).

The Struggle is when you wonder why you started the company in the first place.

The Struggle is when people ask you why you don't quit and you don't know the answer.

The Struggle is when your employees think you are lying and you think they may be right.

The Struggle is when food loses its taste.

The Struggle is when you don't believe you should be CEO of your company.

The Struggle is when you know that you are in over your head and you know that you cannot be replaced.

The Struggle is when everybody thinks you are an idiot, but nobody will fire you.

The Struggle is where self-doubt becomes self-hatred.

The Struggle is when you are having a conversation with someone and you can't hear a word that they are saying because all you can hear is the Struggle.

The Struggle is when you want the pain to stop.

The Struggle is unhappiness.

The Struggle is when you go on vacation to feel better and you feel worse.

The Struggle is when you are surrounded by people and you are all alone.

The Struggle has no mercy.

The Struggle is the land of broken promises and crushed dreams.

The Struggle is a cold sweat.

The Struggle is where your guts boil so much that you feel like you are going to spit blood.

The Struggle is not failure, but it causes failure.

Especially if you are weak. Always if you are weak.

Most people are not strong enough.

Every great entrepreneur, from Steve Jobs to Mark Zuckerberg, went through The Struggle and struggle they did, so you are not alone. But that does not mean that you will make it. You may not make it. That is why it is The Struggle. The Struggle is where true greatness comes from.

But cheer up! I have good news for you—we can foresee all these challenges and prepare for them!

At this point, if you are feeling discouraged, you are not the only one. I received this feedback from almost each one of my beta readers. It is intentional. It is a splash of cold water on your face—hope you are awake now! We have listed all the challenges. Each one of these can be managed. The risk from each one of these can be minimised or nullified. We need to focus and put our effort into mitigating these risks, and overcoming these challenges.

In the rest of the book, you will learn how to prepare for these challenges.

Remember, my goal is to make you realise what it means to venture out as an entrepreneur and make you successful.

Recap

Let's face the reality first: Entrepreneurship is hard. The chances that you will fail are high. Startups fail due to multiple business reasons: not having the right product, a weak team, negative bank balance, competition, and the legal system.

On top of this, you face a high personal risk. Your bank balance might run out, your lifestyle will suffer, your career might take a hit, and you might face social ridicule.

There is no rational reason to be an entrepreneur. It is a struggle. Be ready for it.

I hope I have given you enough of a reality check. My purpose is not to demotivate you or stop you from starting a new business. My purpose is to tell you the truth, so you can prepare for it and start strong!

Finally . . .

"Wannabe" entrepreneur in school or college: Dude, entrepreneurship is not all glamour and money. It comes with real pain. But you know what—you are lucky. I envy you. Because you have TIME on your side. You have YOUTH on your side. You have ENERGY on your side. I suggest you be aware of these risks. Prepare for it. But do NOT quit (yet).

"Friday-night-after-two-drinks" reluctant entrepreneur in your 20s/30s: Let's be sober. Do you understand these risks? Maybe these are the reasons you never do anything. That's okay. I suggest you continue reading. The next chapter is the real deal-breaker for you.

"Ready to go" soon-to-be entrepreneur: Did you consider these scenarios? If yes, are you prepared well enough? If not, you need to prepare NOW. I suggest you finish this book ASAP and start acting on it immediately. You do not have time to lose.

"Already on the train, but less than 12 months" entrepreneur: Did you consider these scenarios? Have you experienced some of these already? How are you dealing with these situations? What are you doing well? What can you change or improve on? Think, reflect.

Loved ones of any of the above (boyfriend, girlfriend, parents, etc.): I am hoping that by now, I am your best buddy! I have given you enough food for thought. Talk to your friend/daughter/son. Understand their perspective. Be in the listening mode. Do not jump to "help." Continue reading the book to ask the right questions.

A real/aspiring VC/Angel investor who has never built a business: I hope you have a better understanding of the struggle. Life is not easy for an entrepreneur. So, stop frowning if you see an aspiring one spamming your email with his or her pitch. Stop frowning if a team misses out one little detail in their presentation. Be patient. You have to ask the right questions. Keep reading the book to understand what these might be.

CHAPTER TWO

Understand Your "Why"

"I WANT TO BE RICH", "I WANT TO
SOLVE A PROBLEM", OR "I JUST WANT
TO GET RID OF MY BOSS"

My biggest mistake as an entrepreneur was I did not know why I wanted to start up.

When I landed in Delhi after quitting my job in Brussels, I was often asked by relatives and friends: Why did you quit a well-paying job and decide to start your own company? My cool-sounding (at least to me) answer then was: "I am motivated by the sense of adventure in doing something new and offbeat. I just want to do it. It is better to fail, then to not try."

Brave words. But looking back, I do not think I was clear in my mind. I never thought it through: about why was I always keen on starting up. What was I looking for from a startup? What type of company did I want to create?

In retrospect, it was a huge mistake. The sense of adventure died out quickly. Over time, I realised I had created a business which did not interest me. I got bored and lost my energy. I lost my entrepreneurial spirit and the desire to keep going.

Why is the "Why?" important?

John Hanc is a famous writer. He has written fourteen books on endurance training and long distance running. Here is what he has to say about running a marathon: (http://www.johnhanc.com/)

"I've learned that finishing a marathon is not just an athletic achievement. It is a state of mind; a state of mind that says anything is possible."

Entrepreneurship is similar to running a marathon—long and painful—where state of mind matters more than state of body.

Your "Why?" is the key to a positive state of mind when you are running the entrepreneurial marathon. It keeps you motivated on a day-to-day basis.

Your "Why?" will help you stick to the fight when you are hit the hardest.

Consider this: You wake up one morning, tired, yet excited. Yesterday was a big day. Your company launched its very first product! In order to generate a (hopefully) positive buzz around it, you invited a leading technology blogger to review the product.

The blogger published his review this morning. The review does not look good by any measure. It will be a big setback to your venture.

You are shocked. Disappointed. You feel cheated. You, along with your team, had invested months of sweat and blood to build this product. All that hard work and sacrifice now seem for nothing.

As a founder, how do you personally recover from this disastrous situation?

You "trick" your mind into getting back up and being energetic again by remembering your "Why?" Why did you start a business? What did you want from your business? Is it important enough for you to get up and try again?

Knowing your "Why?" will help you make the difficult decisions in your entrepreneurial journey.

Consider another scenario. Let us say an investor is willing to put in badly needed funds into your venture, provided you change the product direction significantly. If you compromise and accept the changes, you will not be able to achieve your vision for the product—but this will save your company. If you stick to your ground and refuse the changes (and funds) your company might have to shut down in a month.

How will you react to this situation? Will you make a compromise or stick to your ground? As a founder, you will face many such delicate choice points.

Your "Why?" will eventually serve as the motivation for your employees, providing a bigger purpose and goal for their work.

Finally, as your company grows in size, your personal "Why?" is what will help shape the "vision" for the company.

In his book, "*Start With Why*", Simon Sinek (Sinek, 2011) summarises it beautifully:

"Any person or organisation can explain what they do; some can explain how they are different or better; but very few can clearly articulate why . . .WHY is the thing that inspires us and inspires those around us."

As a founder, you will have to build a team of people who believe in you and your vision. "What" you are doing, and "How" you are doing it will not matter beyond a point. You might be working on the coolest product or the most difficult problem. Unless you define a bigger motivating goal, people will lose the interest and motivation to work with you.

So, why do entrepreneurs start up?

Researchers have spent a lot of time on this topic.

The Enterprise Research Centre, U.K. categorised the motivations for entrepreneurship (Ute Stephan, M. H.C. February, 2015. Understanding Motivations for Entrepreneurship: A review of Recent Research Evidence.) into seven dimensions, the first four being the most common:

1. Achievement, challenge, and learning, e.g. having meaningful work and responsibility, or fulfilling one's personal vision
2. Independence and autonomy, i.e. control over one's own time and work, making independent decisions, flexibility to combine work with one's personal life
3. Income security and financial success
4. Recognition and status
5. Family (tradition/legacy) and roles
6. Dissatisfaction (with prior work arrangement)
7. Community and social motivations, i.e. desire to contribute back to the community through philanthropy or the business itself

In "The Nordic Entrepreneur" survey, 47% entrepreneurs said that they were motivated by a strong need to realise own ideas on how to improve an existing service, solution, or process. The second most popular reason to start up was the desire to stay independent. (http://www.ey.com/Publication/ vwLUAssets/EY-Entrepreneurship-Barometer-2015/$FILE/ EY-Entrepreneurship-Barometer-2015.pdf).

In order to arrive at my own conclusions, I talked to several entrepreneurs—both existing and aspiring ones. Below I summarise the most common reasons for youngsters wanting to start up.

1. "One night stand reasons": I hate my job/boss, I want to have an adventure, etc.
2. I want to create impact and solve a complex/real problem.
3. I want greater autonomy and control.
4. I want money and recognition.

1. "One night stand reasons": I hate my job/boss, I want to have an adventure

"Is desh ka graduate jab apni 9 to 5 job se bore hone lagte hain, to bahar nikalne ke unhe teen raaste soojhte hain. MBA, IAS, Startup"

("When a graduate in this country gets bored with his 9 to 5 job, he thinks of three roads to exit: MBA, IAS, Startup")

– TVF Qtiyapa (https://tvfplay.com/)

Each Friday evening, after a week of putting up with long hours, annoying managers, and irritating colleagues, groups of friends sit down in bars across the country—in Bengaluru, Hyderabad, Mumbai, Pune, Delhi, Gurgaon—and after a few drinks, here is how the conversations often go:

"I am so bored with my job."

"We need to do something. We are wasting our lives here!"

"I hate my boss. He is always finding fault with me!"

"Enough of this slavery! Let's start something of our own."

"Did you hear? Sharmaji's son just raised 10 million dollars at a 100 million valuation!"

"Man, people are playing in millions. We are stuck here, barely able to afford this beer."

Hundreds of new "intentions" to start up are launched every Friday evening over drinks. Most of them fizzle out by Monday morning when the office routine strikes.

["Friday-night-after-two-drinks" reluctant entrepreneur in your 20s/30s: Does this sound familiar?]

If you think your current job is boring, consider a typical day of a startup founder.

- Call the lawyer to get the latest company registration papers
- Call the bank to open your account
- Get stamp papers to sign your lease deed
- Conduct ten interviews to hire a developer
- Send reminders to five investors
- Conduct training sessions for new hires
- Prepare an offer letter for a potential hire
- Make changes to your investor pitch deck . . . and so on.

Where is the fun-filled and challenging work? Maybe a few hours a day, if you get lucky. On the contrary, most founders end up doing work they hate, work they would not do in a normal job setting.

Akshat Choudhary (BlogVault and ActivMob) tells me about his struggle with being a founder.

"I think the biggest difference is I have to do things which

I am not comfortable doing. There is no choice, so I have to do it. For example, I need to do sales or hire for roles which I don't understand. I need to critique work done by others where I am not the expert. But this is all new to me."

Also, being the founder or the CEO does not mean you will have no bosses. There are always bosses. In reality, you come last. Your employee can leave you and move to another company within a day. Your investors can scream at you for results. Your customers will make you wait for hours outside their offices.

Friendly advice: Don't do it for the wrong reasons.

If you are dissatisfied with your job or your boss, maybe you just need to find another job.

If Sharmaji's son has just landed a big funding for his startup, maybe you need to just forget him and focus on your own career.

Don't start up just because it sounds cool or exciting—the sense of adventure dies out quickly, and plenty of mundane tasks comprise a founder's day to day job. In a startup, the founder comes last and must answer to customers, investors and even employees; plus you have to work harder, longer hours.

2. I want to create impact and solve a complex/real problem

To make money, every business tries to solve a problem for the customer.

Thomas Edison, the inventor of the light bulb and regarded as one of the greatest inventors of the twentieth century, wrote,

"I never perfected an invention that I did not think about in terms of the service it might give others. . . I find out what

the world needs, then I proceed to invent. . ." (http://www.
thomasedison.com/quotes.html)

Most of the entrepreneurs I spoke to were clear that
solving a real problem or creating impact was the single biggest
motivating factor for them to start up.

Srikrishnan Ganesan (Twitter @srikrishnang and Founder,
Konotor) (Ganesan, 2016) is a serial entrepreneur and a well-
known force in the startup circles of Chennai. He co-founded
Konotor, a mobile-user engagement platform that helps businesses
engage, retain, and sell more to their mobile app users. Konotor
was acquired by Freshdesk, where the product was re-launched
as hotline.io Prior to starting Konotor, he had built PhonOn, a
mobile social app enabling new rich communication experiences.
He is an alumnus of the Indian Institute of Management Bangalore
(IIMB) and Anna University, Chennai. In his own words:

". . .motivation was definitely about solving real problems
and creating impact. It was also partly driven by coming together
with friends who were ready to take the plunge and landing on
an idea we believed had great potential."

Mohan Rajagopalan (Yaap.io) has a very similar DNA to
Akshat. He is also a true engineer, both at heart and by training.
To quote him:

"I wanted to work on interesting, transformative problems
without big company baggage. I was fascinated by the
opportunity to create a research lab like environment. It may
sound cliché, but it was never about the money . . . it was about
doing it right, and being the best at what we do . . ."

Sangeet (Platformation Labs) was keen on articulating and
solving an intellectual problem based on a fundamental shift
happening in the industry.

"It's easy to become a subject matter expert but I believe it's rare to develop an entirely new lens through which you can see and analyse social and economic systems. I quit and started this full time only because I believed I had developed an entirely new lens that had immense replicability across problem spaces."

Suhani Mohan is the co-founder of Saral Designs. She is working towards providing access to affordable and quality menstrual hygiene products to low-income women in India. She is an alumnus of IIT Bombay, an India Africa Young Visionary (2014), and an Acumen India Fellow (2015) (Mohan, 2016).

Suhani saw a big problem with women's hygiene in rural India.

"While I was working as an investment banker, I had a chance to meet Mr. Anshu Gupta from Goonj. He described how women in rural India use newspapers, rags and other unhygienic methods during their menstruation. I felt deeply ashamed. It had never crossed my mind that when I spend Rs100/month to manage my menstruation, how would a woman, whose entire family's earning is lesser than Rs.1000/month, manage hers. This was when I decided that I must give my fullest to something I believe in and be the change I wish to see."

Kunal Gandhi, Founder, LogicRoots (Gandhi, 2016), is motivated by the sheer impact of building a business in solving problems for customers and creating employment. LogicRoots helps kids get twenty times more math practice through gamification and technology. They have designed original math board games and an award-winning app to help kids practice more math. Kunal has previously worked at McKinsey & Company and is an alumnus of the Indian Institute of Management (IIM)

Ahmedabad and Indian Institute of Technology (IIT) Mumbai (Gandhi, 2016).

"When I started, the main motivation was the thrill of building a business. I would think about possible impact I can have—on my customers and employees. Money was the second motivator."

Brij Bhushan is the co-founder at Magicpin (Bhushan). Magicpin is a hyperlocal startup, which captures interactions and transactions across users and merchants in a locality. Prior to this, Brij worked at Nexus Venture Partners, a VC firm. He also worked at Bain & Company and UrbanTouch. He is an alumnus of the Indian Institute of Management (IIM) Bangalore.

"I had worked prior to Nexus Venture Partners at a startup as an early team member and that was the part of my professional career that I had enjoyed the most. The thrill of building something from scratch—product, team and a business—is unmatched. And with a bit of luck, there is massive upside of creating something that has huge impact."

Are you passionate about solving a particular problem? Does this problem keep you awake at night? Have you been thinking about it for weeks, months, or even years?

Share your problem statement with me on Twitter (@ pango). If you haven't solved it yet, let us think about it together.

Friendly advice: Follow your efforts, not just a passion

People are "passionate" about sports, movies, social work, or entrepreneurship.

But should you follow your passion in entrepreneurship? Not if it is without efforts.

Among entrepreneurs, Mark Cuban is one of my personal favourites. He is a billionaire entrepreneur who made his money by selling Broadcast.com to Yahoo! I subscribe to his advice to aspiring entrepreneurs:

"Don't follow your passion. Follow your efforts."

What matters is the effort you put in, not your passion about anything. On his blog, he concludes, (Cuban, M. "Don't Follow Your Passion, Follow Your Effort." March 18, 2012. http://blogmaverick.com/2012/03/18/dont-follow-your-passion-follow-your-effort/)

"1. When you work hard at something, you become good at it.

2. When you become good at doing something, you will enjoy it more.

3. When you enjoy doing something, there is a very good chance you will become passionate or more passionate about it.

4. When you are good at something, passionate and work even harder to excel and be the best at it, good things happen."

Divakar is the co-founder of Alohomora Education, a non-profit focused on building digital literacy to help children become independent learners who can make well-informed life choices. He is an IIT Madras and IIM Lucknow alumnus. (Sankhla, 2016)

Post Engineering and MBA, Divakar worked in the corporate world for about five years. His passion for teaching led him to take a sabbatical from Citibank and pursue a fellowship with Teach For India. Post fellowship, he continued on in the social sector and channelled his passion into solving the problem of making available practical education to under-privileged children.

Sangeet (Platformation Labs) has an interesting take on the topic of passion.

"I've always believed that passion is not something you are excited about, it is something you are willing to suffer for. I was ready to suffer for this in order to see this succeed . . ."

Follow your effort. It will lead you to your passions and to success.

Friendly advice: Decide on a timeframe

Problem solvers are curious minds. They have the gift of spotting problems and solving them. This gift can also get them in trouble. They are often fragile and face the risk of losing interest in one problem and moving on to another.

Pick a problem that is challenging enough to sustain your interest for an extended duration and keeps you motivated through the non-sexy work required to build a company. Be careful of temporary excitement. A good thumb rule is to mull over the problem for a week. If you are still interested in the problem, this could be the real thing.

Most importantly, give yourself the right timeframe to work it out. Before you start, understand how much time you have. Decide you are not going to quit before that. Set the right expectations.

3. I want greater autonomy and control

As founder and/or CEO, you often have more freedom to decide what you want to work on, whom you want to work with, and when you want to work. You can control (to some extent) the company culture or the working environment, working to the rhythm of your own inspiration or creativity, and deciding your own working hours according to your own energy levels or family obligations.

This can be a great motivating factor.

Mukul Sachan is the co-founder and COO of LendingKart. LendingKart uses analytics and online data to determine whether it wants to lend to businesses. It is one of the fintech success stories in India, having raised $10 million in Series A and $32 million in Series B. Mukul is an ex-ISRO scientist, ex-CFO, and now an entrepreneur. He is an alumnus of IIM Bangalore (Sachan, 2016)

"In my earlier job as a CFO, I realised that I can deliver results on almost all the aspects of the business and not just finance. I used to delve into every aspect of business and was able to provide useful contributions there. Also, within finance, I used to manage it as if it is my own business. The high level of ownership helped me to develop confidence that I can manage the things on my own and possibly for much greater eventual reward; and yes the control."

However, it is very important to note here that full independence is a myth.

As I mentioned earlier, being CEO does not mean there are no bosses (or, in other words, no external forces). You never get 100% control. Why? Because you cannot work in a vacuum. Forces above and below you still control your destiny.

Nitesh (Co-Founder, QuantInsti, 2017) is co-founder of a Financial Technology company Quantinsti. Quantinsti was a pioneer in algorithmic trading in India. Nitesh soon realised that professional freedom is a misnomer.

"People often think that as an entrepreneur, you have full professional freedom. This notion cannot be any farther from the truth! You've to be ready to do any kind of work that business needs and keep your 'interests' on the side. This was exact opposite of what I used to think when we were starting."

At the highest level, you are controlled by the social and economic structure. Is the macro economy doing well? Can you easily do business in your country? Is the taxation system favourable?

You are controlled by your customers. Do they like your product? Would they buy? Do they have money to buy?

Next, investors control you. Will they put in cash into your business? What will their expectations be?

Finally, your team controls you. Will they put in their share of the effort? Will they be committed? For how long?

Friendly advice: Define your "no-compromise" rules

If you started (or are starting) a business to have greater control, you must get that control to stay motivated.

Decide on what you consider the most important desires in your life. Set "no-compromise" rules around these desires. Here are some examples:

- No compromise on quality of product
- Veto on all new hires
- Innovate constantly
- Always look out for the customer
- No work from 5 p.m. to 8 p.m., so that you spend time with your family
- No work on Sunday morning and afternoon

You will be tempted to break these rules several times. If you persist, you will win. You will feel happy, satisfied, and continue to stay motivated on your entrepreneurial journey.

4. I want money and recognition

"The business of business is to make money."

Let's face it—several entrepreneurs start up, simply because they believe it will allow them to make big bucks—a lot more than the slow trickle from a steady job.

Ask yourself: are you in it for the money?

Do you check your bank balance weekly? Are you driven by maximising it, day after day, month after month, year after year?

Do you look for creative ways to invest your money and multiply it further? Do you get a kick when the stock you bought goes up by 50% in a year? Do you lose sleep when you lose money in any investment?

Do you like what money can buy—a sea facing apartment, luxury car, international travel, premium furniture?

Do you not care about the quality of your work, as long as it makes money for you? Are you happy to build a silly app if it makes money?

Friendly advice: If you are chasing money, go where it is.

It's perfectly OKAY to be driven by money—greed is good. If you are looking for money, be very clear about it in your head. Do not confuse yourself by looking for a "big" or "cool" problem to solve. You are an opportunist, not a solution seeker. If a silly app sending cute cat pics every hour has the potential to make you thousands or millions, that's what you should be working on!

Friendly advice: Understand opportunity cost and risk reward balance

While thinking about your financial future in a startup,

make sure you remember that you will take home little to no salary in the first few years, until (if) you hit it big, and that there is the opportunity cost of leaving a steady, well-paying job for a higher risk option.

Consider you have two options in front of you: A: Continue in your job with salary of INR 5 million and B: Start a new business with a projected cash flow of INR X for you (not for the company).

Since all you care about is money, you should evaluate Option A vs. Option B only on financial terms. Starting a new business should give you a long-term financial gain that is at least equal to your current job's salary. X should be greater than INR 5 million. Every time you make less than this amount, you lose money.

It is not a simple concept. You might be earning INR 2 million in your own company and feel happy about it. In reality, you are losing INR 3 million compared to your maximum earning potential. If you just care for money, you should be working in a job, unless you can earn more than INR 5 million in your startup.

In fact, you should be earning more than INR 5 million to compensate for the additional risk you are taking in a startup. The risk and reward should balance out. Entrepreneurship is higher risk, so financial rewards should be higher.

Answering the "Why": Understanding your goals

Now that you know some of the reasons that drive other entrepreneurs to startup, take some time to understand what your own motivations are.

What are your needs and desires? What excites you? What motivates you to work hard and put in late hours?

What does your ego want? When does your ego feel happy?

Why would you take the pain? What justifies this journey? Are you ready to suffer to see it succeed?

These difficult questions are at the crux of your entrepreneurial journey. Understanding your own goals is not easy. No matter what you think, you never know enough about yourself.

I would suggest an honest reflection. Listen to your ego, while shutting out your brain for this exercise. Let your ego tell you what you want, instead of your brain dictating what you should want. What does your ego tell you? What will make your ego happy?

One trick I recommend is to build imaginary worlds and then consider: would you be happy in these worlds?

Here are some examples to get you started.

Imagine yourself working on solving a big problem that matters to you. This problem could be related to engineering or be a technical one (how about taking humans to Mars, or growing crops on Mars?); or it could be social (how to build cheap houses in cities? How to make solar power cheaper?). And now, you have solved it! Your solution works for thousands and millions of customers. It has dramatically changed their lives. Hurray! But nobody knows you are the one who has solved the problem, nor do you end up making millions. Will this situation make your ego happy?

Or how about this: Imagine you are a freelancer web designer. You have a good reputation in the online communities. Clients like your work and come back to you. You have a good, steady stream of income, enough for you to lead a comfortable life, but not enough to make you super rich. You have total control over your life over what you do, how much you work, when you work, whom you work with. You can take vacations when you want. You can move to another city or country, if you wish. You are the ultimate practitioner of *"The 4-Hour Workweek" made famous by Tim* Ferriss (Ferriss, 2009). Will this situation make your ego happy?

Imagine you are a stock trader. Your life revolves around your next trade, your next profit, or your next loss. All you talk about is cash. You do not care if this is the most boring job ever, as long as you make money. You dream of swimming in a pool of gold coins, like Uncle Scrooge. Your nightmares are about the stock market crashing, leading to huge losses for you. You are excited about spending money on the next watch, next smartphone, or the next big house. You show off your wealth—making sure everybody else knows you are successful and filthy rich. Will this situation make your ego happy?

Imagine you have won a lottery. This lottery is different though. It does not give you cash. It gives you the power to tick items off your bucket list. So, you want to go visit fifty countries; this lottery will make it happen. You want to bungee jump? This lottery will arrange for it. You want to run a marathon? This lottery will help you train for it. The ticket is like a genie. You do not make a lot of money out of it. Nobody knows about it. Will this situation make your ego happy?

I can think of many more situations like these. Take time to find your goals.

Be honest with yourself. Be selfish—it is about you.

It is okay to be confused. Do I want to solve this problem,

or make money, or both? Cannot make up your mind? That's okay. Take your time.

It is also okay to change. Your needs and desires keep changing. So can your goals. Your goal might be autonomy today, money tomorrow. Do not be inflexible.

Finally, prioritise. You cannot have ten goals.

Here is a tip: follow Warren Buffet's 25/5 rule. Write down twenty-five things you want from your life. Choose the top five. Forget about rest. Focus on achieving the five.

Once you find your goals, write them down. Post it at your desk, in clear sight, and review them weekly, if not daily. Do not forget.

There might be faster ways to achieve your goals: Is the gain worth the pain?

Hopefully by reading so far, you have given thoughts to what the driving force and goals are, behind your desire to start up. You likely also understand well enough how a startup is likely to change your life in ways you may not have considered earlier. And still you have made peace with the pain. You are raring to go.

Allow me to throw one more wrench into your plans.

When I started my company, my first real learning was that progress takes time—a lot of it. Everything is so sloooowwww.

And the list goes on and on . . .

In my conversations with entrepreneurs on skills required to succeed as an entrepreneur, the most common answer was patience.

Kunal Gandhi (LogicRoots) comes from consulting world, where things move fast. You get used to tight deadlines, overnight work, rapid progress, and results. You get used to the adrenaline rush. Coming into the startup world, the realities hit Kunal pretty hard. Patience was the hardest lesson for him to learn. He recalls his experiences:

" . . .Almost everything takes much longer than I thought. I realised that the journey from conceptualizing a product to revenue is not just the time it takes to build the first product. Instead it also includes the years that go into making hundreds of mistakes and the money that goes into creating features that no one wants. It is also the hours that go into building seemingly useless relationships that come in handy 4 years down the line. It also includes the months spent in training a team member to do your role which you yourself could have done a lot faster.

All this takes time. But fresh out of a job, I did not have the patience for all this. It was hard."

His advice to young entrepreneurs?

"Patience. It takes longer than you think. Cannot be done in 2 years. Start small and take it up slow. Enjoy the process not just the outcome."

If there were a marathon of patience, good entrepreneurs would win.

Why so? Well, let us look at some situations every budding entrepreneur goes through:

You try to build your product. Your lead developer runs away to another company. The system breaks down. All hell is let loose.

You try to hire people. After going through hundreds of resumes, you short-list three candidates. You interview them. You like one of them. You "date" this candidate for some time, take them for dinner to one of the best restaurants, and finally make an offer. The prospective employee chokes as if you have asked them to work for free and wants double the salary you offered, with a "co-founder" title and 20% equity. You feel stupid. After multiple rounds of negotiations, the person agrees and asks you to wait for a day for the final answer. The next thing you know—this person has used your offer to get a raise in the existing job and dumps you. You feel like an idiot. The process re-starts. After struggling for another three or four months, you settle on an "average" person who joins you, but cannot make progress at the rate you want. Your product release is delayed. You can do nothing, but hope and pray for another candidate.

You try to sell your product. You meet an alumnus of your school, a senior guy, while at your customer's. He promises to help you. You write him an email. He forwards the email to "X" two levels down. X has no interest in helping you. He gives you an appointment for next month. He just keeps finding new ways to block you. Finally, you get his approval after a couple of months. Now you have to deal with the finance department to get your commercial agreement. It takes months. At last, the product is launched. Then you wait for your payment. . . *"chakkar pe chakkar"* (the hamster wheel of entrepreneurship)

You try to raise funding. You look for contacts in the VC community. You pitch to twenty VCs. Some like your idea, some do not understand it (and pretend they do not like it). Among those who like it, only a couple of them want to move forward. One of them sends you a term sheet, followed by a long and painful negotiation process. Six months pass. Term sheet is signed. Where is the cash? You wait another couple of months to get it.

Such stories are common. Entrepreneurs start with the adrenaline flowing through their blood and an attitude of *"Kar le duniya mutthi mein"* (loosely translated to "the world in your pocket"). And then the realities hit them. It is difficult to get anything done in the real world. You are exposed to an outside world where you have little control, a world that is slow and hostile. It will frustrate you. It will suck away your energy.

Akshat Choudhary (BlogVault and ActivMob) reflects on his experiences. He says,

"Things take time to happen. Sometimes it is just a matter of "right time". So be patient and chip away at the problem. If you are solving a real need, things will fall into place eventually."

Do you have enough patience to stay long enough in the game and not quit too soon?

Do you need to start a new business to achieve your goals? Or is there a faster and an easier path?

What are your alternate options? I will consider three, but there might be more.

Option 1: You can join a big company.

Option 2: You can join a mid-size growing startup.

Option 3: You can join a small startup which is still figuring it out.

Now I create a plot. On the X-axis is your "Gain", which indicates how successful you are in achieving your goals. On the Y-axis is your "Pain". This pain reflects the risk you are taking and all the struggles you might face—which we discussed in the previous chapter.

The map will look something like the one below.

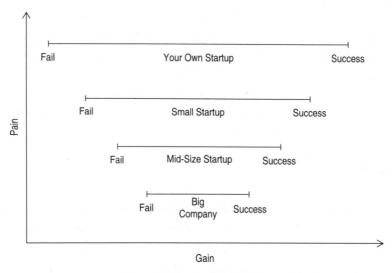

Figure 2: Pain vs. Gain Equation

Where do you want to be? What is your risk tolerance?
Small gain, but small pain?
Large gain, but large pain and large risk?

I am not discouraging you from entrepreneurship. What I am asking you to do is to think hard about what it means to be an entrepreneur and what you can get out of it. Depending on what you want to accomplish, starting up may not be the most optimal choice. Think about the above chart again and again.

Recap

A startup is like a marathon—long and painful—where state of mind matters. As a startup founder, you need a strong "Why", a strong reason to keep going in the toughest times, make difficult decisions, and find the bigger purpose for your venture. Beware of "One night stand", weak "Whys" such as "I hate my boss", or "I want to have an adventure". These weak whys do not last. Try to understand your real motivation: Is it to solve a complex problem? Is it independence? Is it money and recognition?

Finally, remember there might be easier ways to achieve your goals. A startup is probably the most difficult path. Clearly understand the Pain vs. Gain equation.

Finally . . .

If you are a . . .

"Wannabe" entrepreneur in school or college: First, are you clear on your goals? Still confused? That's okay. But keep thinking. Know before you start.

"Friday-night-after-two-drinks" reluctant entrepreneur in your 20s/30s: You are the one I am the most concerned about. Do you know your goals? Or are you still confused by the wrong reasons? Make up your mind. You can probably achieve your goals in other ways with less pain. Starting a business might not be the best option for you. If you think it is—get serious and prepare.

"Ready to go" soon-to-be entrepreneur: Did you consider other options to achieve your goals? I do not want to confuse you, but it is something for you to keep in mind. Prepare mentally.

"Already on the train, but less than 12 months" entrepreneur: I hope you know your goals. Do you remember them? Please write them down somewhere. Are you moving towards them? Have they changed? Spend some time thinking about your goals tonight.

Loved ones of any of the above (boyfriend, girlfriend, parents, etc.): Ask this question: "What are your goals?" Push back and challenge. Make sure he or she is not solving temporary problems. Help him or her understand other options.

A real/aspiring VC/Angel investor who has never built a business: Before you evaluate the business idea, evaluate the founder. Understand the founder's goals and motivations. An average idea with a super clear motivated founder is better than the best of business ideas in the hands of a confused founder. Talk to founders and try to understand: Has the founder faced any struggles in her or his career? How did they deal with it? What did they learn? Are they solid in their heart and soul (not just brains)? Choose the founder first, then the idea.

CHAPTER THREE

How to Generate Business Ideas?

**"I WOULD START TOMORROW, IF ONLY
I HAD A NEW BUSINESS IDEA!"**

When working as a consultant in Brussels, Belgium, I was given a Blackberry (back in 2007, a cool device and probably the smartest phone around) for professional calls and emails. It was awesome. I loved getting my emails on my phone . . . until I came to India on vacation. Mobile data connectivity in India (back then) was poor—spotty and expensive! I just could not use the push email service.

This was our business idea! After I experienced the problem first-hand, my co-founder and I saw an opportunity to provide push email service over SMS (no data required). It was the first product we built and a very successful one.

Am I a genius for coming up with the idea? No.

If I had not used the Blackberry, or come to India on vacation, or visited a place with poor mobile connectivity, none of this might have happened. Of course, we can all connect the dots and create a magical story out of it. In reality, we just observed what bothered us.

I would start tomorrow, if only
I had a good business idea!

Have you heard yourself or your friend complaining?

> "I will start as soon as I find the next billion dollar killer idea"
>
> "I want to start something of my own, but I don't know what to do."
>
> "I am not creative enough to generate ideas."
>
> "Every idea I think of—somebody is already doing it. I just cannot find a unique idea."

Are you stuck in the dark zone of "I don't have a business idea"? Is it your favourite excuse of not doing anything?

It is not your fault. You likely think it is too complex to come up with a business idea. You probably have a misconception of what a business idea is. Popular startup stories tell a business idea is something revolutionary changing the face of the earth. Or maybe you think an idea will just strike your mind when all the stars align on one fine day.

Let me try and help you solve this problem.

There are two steps to choosing a business idea.

1. Generating new ideas
2. Evaluating them to determine the best to proceed with

In this chapter, we will talk about the first step: how to generate new business ideas and turn you into an idea machine. The next chapter will address how to evaluate your ideas.

Ideas are not magical "a-ha" moments

What is a business idea? In simple words, it is the solution to a problem. When you think of a business idea, you have to think of a problem and its solution.

I recently read a story about how a waffle iron inspired Nike's shoes.

From Business Insider: "Nike co-founder Bill Bowerman was having breakfast with his wife one morning in 1971 when it dawned on him that the grooves in the waffle iron she was using would be an excellent mould for a running shoe"

What would be a typical popular media interpretation of this idea?

- "This was a revolutionary idea."
- "Bill was a genius. Only he could have come up this idea."
- "It all happened in one magical "a-ha" moment."

Not completely false, but not completely true either.

Here's what happened: Bowerman spent nearly a decade studying jogging best practices, making improvements to athletic footwear designs, and even co-writing a book on running. This was all years BEFORE he had this idea. He teamed up with a business partner who had a Master's in business and knew the running shoe market. The two of them earned $3 million selling shoes before designing even one of their own and starting the business we now know as Nike.

You might have your own picture of "magic" happening . . . almost like a scene out of a movie. There is a guy strolling in a park, or sitting under a tree, or in his shower—and—bam!—an idea hits him. And off he goes to start building a business out of it the very next day, and the next thing you know—he is a billionaire. What a fairy tale!

Popular folklore ignores the details—by design, on purpose. A magical "a-ha" moment is a much better story than "worked on a topic for 5 years before coming up with the idea".

How to generate ideas

Most ideas come out of deep observations and experience— personal or professional—over a long period of time. The experiences allow you to connect different dots and find new solutions.

Let us look at some techniques we can use to start to generate more ideas by spotting problems:

1. Problems faced by you (or friends/family) in your day-to-day life
2. Problems faced at work or in your area of interest
3. Problems being solved in other parts of the world
4. Problems faced by companies leading the latest trend

1. Problems faced by you (or friends/family) in your day-to-day life

Do you have a tendency to constantly complain about the world? Do you see a new problem daily in your life? Are you generally dissatisfied with products you use and services you receive?

When you find your mind complaining about something, listen to it carefully. It has identified a problem. Now all you need is to figure out the solution! Jot down the problem right away!

Is your mind saying something like, "I wonder why we never do it this way?" Ah-ha! Jot that down too. You never know what may come of it in the next few days or weeks, when you add information, data, ideas, and solutions.

Back in 2008, four students were distraught with expensive eyewear. They wanted to change their glasses, but could not. They could not believe that eyewear was so expensive. They wanted to disrupt the eyewear market in the same way Zappos had disrupted the footwear market. Initially, when they shared the idea with friends, it was received with scepticism. But the students persisted. They launched the company Warby Parker. The rest is history. Warby Parker has been one of the brightest success stories of ecommerce in the US market. The founders faced a problem personally and solved it.

The first product of Sabeer Bhatia and Jack Smith, co-founders of Hotmail, was not a web-based email system. It was a web-based personal directory, called JavaSoft. JavaSoft was a weekend and evening project. They had not quit their jobs yet. However, they now faced a problem. Their employer had installed a firewall and they could no longer exchange personal email! They could still access the web through the firewall. So, it meant that if there was web access to personal emails, it could solve the problem! And that's how they arrived at their killer idea: web-based email (Livingston, 2007).

Stephen Kaufer and his wife were trying to plan a vacation in the late nineties. The internet was a new phenomenon then. Their travel agent recommended an island and a resort. Although he looked online for the island, not much information was available. Finally, in an online chat room, he read that the island was not particularly safe! So, he switched the island and hotel. Now he wanted to know more about the quality of the hotel. Nothing came up, except for the glossy hotel website itself. This experience led him to create TripAdvisor, where one could find unbiased opinions about tourist destinations and places (Livingston, 2007).

Sometimes, ideas can come out of looking for solutions to your personal weaknesses.

Did Mark Zuckerberg start Facebook to solve his problem with making friends (as shown in the movie "*The Social Network*")? Did Evan Williams, founder and ex-CEO of Twitter, start Twitter because he is quiet and slow to make decisions?

The Harvard Business Review article, "Mark *Zuckerberg and Misery as Motivation*", *authored by* Rosabeth Moss Kanter (Kanter, n.d.) discusses the phenomenon of entrepreneurship as compensation for personal weaknesses and inner misery.

Kanter writes, "Restless dissatisfaction—that feeling that something isn't quite right—propels entrepreneurship and innovation. Sometimes the motivation is straightforward and doesn't require pop Freudian analysis. Get annoyed about a something that isn't working, and invent a gizmo to fix it. See your mother suffer from cancer, and become a scientist seeking a cure. Get angry about the sorry state of urban education, and start an organisation to tackle it. Personal stories lie behind many successful social or business ventures."

The point is to observe your own life carefully. Observe what bothers you, what hurts you—your business opportunity may be right under your nose just waiting to be discovered!

2. Problems faced at work or in your area of interest

Each one of us has an area of interest or work. If you are a researcher, you have an area of specialisation. If you are employed, you work for a company which solves a problem for its customers. You might probably have other interest areas, such as music, sports, literature, or travel.

Can you find a problem in your area of interest or work?

Siddhartha Agrawal (Wallsoft Labs) worked in a scientific computing services company in New Delhi. As the business development lead, his job was to talk to customers, to understand what their pain points were, and to understand if they were getting what they wanted. That is how he spotted an opportunity! His customers told him they were not happy with what they were getting. Siddhartha believed he could solve their problems in a much better way. He decided to start up.

Chaya Jadhav (VirtualMob) was working with a client when she got the idea of an Augmented Reality (AR) gaming agency.

"I got the idea of AR gaming, because I was consulting some of my clients on new tech trend for digital brands. And AR was something which every brand wanted as their key marketing channel, and not many agencies were in to AR as it was so nascent. We started off as an AR gaming agency, to prove the market and get some real validation. Also to understand how big the market is, we had to manually build AR apps. After a year, we got a good understanding of the pain points of our customers with lots of feedback—which we created or turned into a product."

Even Infosys was founded by N.R. Narayana Murthy and six of his friends, after they resigned from their jobs as software professionals at Patni Computer Systems!

It is easy to get lost in the day-to-day drill of meetings, presentations, and more meetings at the workplace. You forget the bigger picture. Life moves on quickly from weekend to weekend. There are no new ideas, there is no new thinking. You just end up waiting for your next pay raise or promotion.

So, what can you do differently? You can take a **customer-centric view**.

First understand the customer problem your company is solving. Second, understand how customers think and what they want.

You can start doing this right now, in your paycheck job. Here are some examples:

- As a programmer, you are <u>not</u> employed by the company to write code. You were hired to solve one or more <u>customer</u> problems through software!
- If you are a research analyst, you were <u>not</u> hired to build a sophisticated excel worksheet; you were hired to give intelligent and well-analysed answers to your <u>clients'</u> business problems!
- If you are in charge of logistics in a retail company, you were <u>not</u> hired to run logistics; you were hired to ensure the best possible delivery time to your customers.

Next, consider this:

Is your company doing a good job of giving customers what they want?

Can you do it better? Can you do it cheaper? Can you do old things in a new, more efficient way—for your customers?

As an example, customers buying from an e-commerce site would be delighted if they:

1. Get their orders delivered in 24 hours
2. Get what they ordered
3. Can return items with minimal effort
4. Can get refunds instantly **and**
5. Can resolve their problems on a single 10-minute (or less) phone call

If you work for an e-commerce company, is your company delivering on these points of customer delight? Is your competition delivering? Is an e-commerce player anywhere in the world delivering it (if yes, it means it is possible to do it)? Soon, you will find ideas trickling in that may just be good business ideas for your own startup.

Expand your mindset and horizons within your paycheck company. Try to learn more about its products and customers. Talk to customers at every opportunity, if, and when you can. Talk to partners and build your network.

Do not be limited by your job and your function. Learn about other functions needed to get your valuable product or service to the end-user. Talk to people in other departments of the company. (Lunch breaks and before/after meetings can be a great time!). If you are an engineer, learn about marketing and sales. If you are in customer service, talk to product designers. If you are a marketing specialist, always chat with the sales force and the customer service folks.

If you keep your eyes and mind open, your area of work can be a gold mine of business opportunities.

3. Problems being solved in other parts of the world

Are there problems being solved in other parts of the world, but still not being solved in your market?

If you find one such problem, there are multiple advantages to this approach.

First, the idea is already tested out with customers. If something works and sells in one part of the world, it is likely to work in another part of the world. Of course, it may need to be customised to local needs and preferences. There are plenty of examples: fast food chains, clothing brands, and beverages like Coca-Cola.

Second, it is easier to raise funds. Investors love proof of concepts; and what is better than an actual running business! It is much easier to explain and understand "Uber of India", "PayPal of India" when we have its original company as an example.

Snapdeal was launched as the "Groupon" of India. Later it modified its business model to become a true e-commerce player. Jumbo King, a chain of fast food restaurants specialising in *vada pav*, a Mumbai specialty, was inspired by McDonald's and Burger King.

Traditionally, business disruptions have flown from west to east. Recently, however, we are reaching a better balance, with innovations such as low cost smart phones and cash on delivery, starting in the east and expanding to the west.

Pay close attention to global trends—before you know it they will be all the rage locally, and they can be a great opportunity if you act quickly and become a key player in that space.

4. Problems faced by companies leading the latest trend

"In the age of the Gold Rush, it was not the gold diggers, but the tool providers who made real money."

Think about the tools and panning supplies. The food supply. Clothing and heavy work boot sales. Tents and blankets. Food for horses. The list of adjacent businesses to gold mining was long! The need for a wide variety of supplies in that chain created fortunes during the Gold Rush days!

My hometown in India, Kota, is a city known for institutions preparing students for various competitive examinations across India. Back in the early 2000s, the explosion in the number of such institutes and students was just starting to happen. Many institutes came up—some died, but most survived and were successful. But many other people made a lot of money on this wave: homeowners who transformed their houses into "hostels", restaurant owners who started "hostel kitchens", bookshop owners, fruit sellers, movie theatres, etc. The economy of the whole city went up with this wave.

I call this cascading effect "The Tree of Adjacencies."

New trends or waves (internet, mobile, social, e-commerce, Internet of Things, Artificial Intelligence, and so on) create new opportunities. Waves like these also lift up many adjacent businesses.

Let us take the example of e-commerce.

- E-commerce companies need warehousing, logistics, and shipping
- Warehousing companies need real estate, construction, software, and operational support
- Construction companies need cement and labour
- Logistics companies need trucks

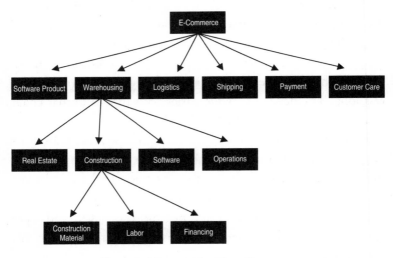

Figure 3: Adjacency Tree for e-Commerce

We have seen logistics companies benefitting from the e-commerce wave. Sahil Barua and Mohit Tandon set up Delhivery as the logistics arm for e-commerce players, and their business has seen tremendous success.

Pick a growing industry/trend and try to understand its complete end-to-end value chain; you might just discover an opening that is waiting for you to step in!

Let's ideate!

If you do not have a business idea yet, work on it actively.

Think revolutionary, but do not forget the evolutionary

There is no dearth of examples of disruptive startups that have revolutionised businesses. Google revolutionised search; Amazon, Flipkart, and Snapdeal revolutionised retail; Uber revolutionised private transportation; and Housing.com and OLX revolutionised the real estate brokering business, just to name a few. Every potential startup founder likely dreams of his or her company being added to this list.

While I encourage you to think big, it is incredibly hard, and frankly a lot of pressure to come up with the "next big **revolutionary** idea". And sometimes unnecessary, too.

Do not forget that your business idea could simply be an **evolutionary** solution to an existing problem. In other words, if you can provide the same or similar product or service, faster, cheaper, or with much better customer experience—you could have a very successful business on your hands in no time.

Look at Apple. Apple did not invent a Walkman (iPod) or a smartphone (iPhone).

The Walkman had existed for a long time. Apple changed the game by launching the iPod. The iPod was several times better than other existing products.

Similarly, smartphones had existed for a long time before the iPhone. Apple changed the game by dramatically improving the user experience with its launch of the iPhone.

Sticking with smartphones, consider Micromax—an Indian low cost smartphone company. It offered similar smartphones that were 20-30% cheaper than the competition. It made owning a smartphone affordable to millions of new customers.

Changing the business model to offer a service at a cheaper cost—does that sound familiar? The Indian software industry is built on this idea. So is the Chinese manufacturing industry.

Look around your neighbourhood or your city. Who are the rich entrepreneurs? You will probably find that they are people in traditional businesses—real estate, clothing, food, and beverages. These people are solving existing problems in different ways. Now, you might decide not to venture into these traditional businesses due to various reasons—and that's okay. But if you make this simple mindset shift from revolutionary to evolutionary, I'll bet your world of opportunities will open up.

Make it a habit

Habits work, resolutions don't. If you are serious about generating ideas, you must make it a habit.

Commit to writing down two new ideas daily into your notebook/notes app. Set up a calendar reminder or download a habit app on your mobile. I use the "Productive" mobile app to build and track habits.

You will get better with time. You will start noticing opportunities around you. Your quality of ideas will improve. Your creativity will start to flow.

Read, read, read

Reading is fuel for the brain. You have to feed your brain with continuous knowledge and research to allow yourself an understanding and appreciation of the possibilities before you.

Develop the habit of reading—everything from business and economy, to blogs by business and management leaders, to the latest industry buzzwords, startup success stories, VC investments, entrepreneur talks, etc.

Read "proactively". Before you read, take some time to reflect on what you already know about the topic—it will help you process and retain what you read significantly better.

Meet people

New thinking can't happen in isolation.

I suggest you build a network of people. Ideally, this network will have people from diverse backgrounds and expertise; people as motivated as you are to start a new business. The more you talk to them, the more you hang out with them—the more you will learn, understand, and expand your thinking.

Talk to entrepreneurs about their experiences, ask them how they came up with an idea, and what problems they faced; find out who their mentors are. Each time you talk to them, or listen to them—you will learn new things, you will learn a new way to think about startups, a new way to think about life.

Recap

Aspiring entrepreneurs get stuck in the dark zone of "I can't think of one good idea to start". There is a way out!

A business idea is a solution to a problem. To generate ideas, you should think about problems. Ideas are not magical "a-ha" moments. Most successful ideas come from years of deep experience and careful observations. Observe:

1. Problems faced by you (or friends/family) in your day-to-day life. Warby Parker's founders were struggling with expensive eyewear themselves.
2. Problems faced at work/in your area of interest. Narayan Murthy realised the opportunity at his job at Patni Computer Systems.
3. Problems being solved in other parts of the world. Snapdeal was inspired from Groupon in the US.
4. Problems faced by companies leading the latest trend. Delhivery came up to improve logistics for ecommerce players.

Often, you are aware of a problem, but try to look for revolutionary solutions. There are many evolutionary solutions available as well. Think about doing things better (iPhone) and/or cheaper (Micromax).

And last, but not least, you have to make ideation a habit. Keep a diary, read, and meet/interact with people.

Finally . . .

If you are a . . .

"Wannabe" entrepreneur in school or college: Start thinking about problems and solutions. Start making it a habit, read, talk, and connect. Finally note it down.

"Friday-night-after-two-drinks" reluctant entrepreneur in your 20s/30s: Use the occasional adrenaline rush to think of ideas. Make a note or you will forget. It is likely you have a job. Focus on problems you are already solving for your customer and how you can do it better.

"Ready to go" soon-to-be entrepreneur: You must have an idea ready by now (hopefully). We will talk about evaluation in the next chapter. Make sure you have evaluated the idea well.

"Already on the train, but less than 12 months" entrepreneur: I would love to hear your story. How did you come up with your idea? Ping me @Pango on Twitter, to share.

Loved ones of any of the above (boyfriend, girlfriend, parents, etc.): You can help generate ideas by thinking about your own experiences. Keep an eye out!

A real/aspiring VC/Angel investor who has never built a business: It is good to understand how an entrepreneur got the idea. Reconstructing the journey from idea to business will help you understand the motivation and execution. Also, think about how you can help the entrepreneur to define the problem statement better and build a better solution.

CHAPTER FOUR

How to Evaluate a Business Idea?

"I LIKE THIS IDEA. LET'S JUST DO IT"

In the last chapter, I shared how I came up with a business idea. But do you know how my co-founder and I decided that our idea was the business idea to start up with?

Here was our evaluation: We personally liked the idea. We asked a couple of our friends, who liked the idea—sort of. And off we went!

I would not recommend this method to you!

How NOT to evaluate a business idea?

Have you ever come up with an idea and felt super excited about it? So excited you decide to start a business immediately?

Have you ever come up with an idea and decided to write a full business plan around it? Then went on to find the best business plan template online and started filling it in?

Both are examples of how NOT to evaluate a business idea.

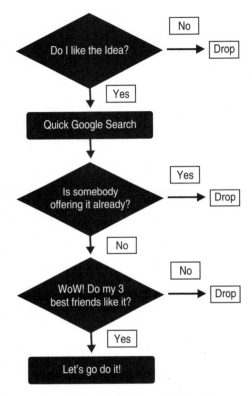

Figure 4: The "Two Minute" Evaluation

1. What is wrong with the "Two-minute evaluation" technique?

To start with, it is based on the preferences of a sample set of ONE customer—YOU. Many times, you might not even be the ideal customer of your business idea. How can you evaluate it?

Research shows that people often under- or overestimate the potential of their own creations (Grant, 2017). Intuition can be your friend if you are working in your area of expertise. If you are a doctor working on a healthcare business idea, that's great! If you are a software engineer working on an application development tool, that's perfect! If you are a sales person working on a sales tool, that's ideal!

But the same intuition can become your enemy when you try to apply it to areas outside your expertise. A doctor working on a retail business idea cannot rely on his gut alone. Neither can a software engineer working on an e-commerce idea or a sales person working on an HR tool.

I am not discounting the power of intuition and gut feeling. These are powerful forces developed from thousands of years of evolution. All I am saying is, you are only one customer. You need a larger customer base to use and buy your product or service. You need real data and feedback to validate your intuition.

2. Write a twenty-page business plan that focuses on investor

Remember the business plan template you learned in your MBA class or from an online tutorial?

Define the product. Show how it plays in a $100 billion market. Describe how you will beat your competition and how great your team is, and explain how you will execute your plan over the next three years. Finally, conclude with a P&L and Cash flow statement for the next five years.

A plan like this can help you get an A grade in an MBA course, or a winning position in a B-Plan competition, but it won't help you find out whether you should invest your life and money into an idea.

Why?

Because it focuses on the investor. It does not focus on you or the customer. These long business plans were designed with the purpose of convincing the investor to put money into your business.

When you have to sell to an investor, what do you do?

First, you show the biggest market possible. If you are selling shoes online, you start with "People in India buy 100s of millions of shoes. Even if we get 5% of that huge market, we are golden." If you are selling groceries online, you start by saying "People in India buy 100s of billions of groceries. Even if we get 1% of that huge market, we are golden," and so on . . . you get it.

Show a huge market and then show your potential share in it as a small percentage—and—done!

Second, if you have to sell it to an investor, you focus on how she can get back her return on investment. You build an awesome revenue and profit projection with huge growth. You show 10, 100, or 1000% growth year after year to justify the investment in your company. You build so many assumptions that you stop caring after a point. You want higher growth? No problem! I will just change an MS Excel cell. Thus, it becomes an Excel modelling exercise.

As an entrepreneur, can you even "imagine" how to capture 2% or 5% of a multi-billion-dollar market? Can you draw an action plan to do it? Most likely, not. Who cares about return on investment even before you start?

How will you get the first 10, 20, 100, or 1000 customers to buy the product? Who are these people? Where are they?

How will you manage this business? How will you execute its operations?

Will it motivate you personally? Does it align with your goals? What will you do on Day One?

The traditional business plan template does not answer these questions enough.

How to evaluate a business idea?

I propose using a simple business plan evaluation template as outlined below.

Answer these questions:

1. Can you identify and profitably serve 100 customers?
2. Can you find the cash to start this business?
3. Can you acquire customers in a sustainable way?
4. Can you execute, i.e., can you transform the idea into business?
5. Does the idea fit with your "Why"?

Why I would recommend this list?

1. It focuses on customers
2. It focuses on cash
3. It focuses on sales
4. It focuses on execution and operations
5. It focuses on you

1. Can you identify and profitably serve 100 customers?

Remind yourself that the goal of a business is to solve a problem for a customer. How do you know that your business idea can achieve this goal?

Your own beliefs and experiences can only go so far. At the same time, you can't possibly talk to thousands of customers and figure out what they want, and whether they will buy your product or not.

What is the right way to go about it?

Focus on a small set of customers, say about 100, evaluate if you are able to solve their problem profitably, and then expand. Do not think about the first thousands or millions of customers right away.

Facebook was created to solve a niche problem: How to enable college students to connect in the best possible way. Its goal was not to connect a billion people. Once it nailed the problem of connecting college students, it expanded to other areas. At last count, it is close to serving two billion people.

If you are building a B2B offering, the initial target could be one customer. Solve the problem for that one customer.

Siddhartha Agrawal (Wallsoft Labs) followed this approach when he built his product around one anchor customer while making sure that product could scale to others later. This is the ultimate idea validation.

"We had an exclusive tie up with a customer before we started. The customer was reasonably large, yet the decision maker was young enough to understand our way of working. The exclusive tie up motivated the customer to help us with the intricacies of capital markets before we designed the system. Further, the problem we were solving was an industry-wide problem, so even if our anchor customer broke our arrangement, we could approach other customers and not face a huge setback."

Chaya Jadhav (VirtualMob) also had customers from Day

One. Her sole focus on Day One was to deliver a service to this customer. Later, she took this service and productised it to expand her reach to new customers.

". . . we had customers from day one as we were an agency for AR apps. And once we took a decision to move from service to a product, it got very intense and challenging . . ."

In order to evaluate your idea with these 100 customers (or one company) in mind, think about the following:

1. Can you define the customer problem? Is it real?
2. How is your solution better than competition?
3. Are your target customers willing to buy? At what price? Is it profitable? Is this price higher than your cost?

Can you define the customer problem? Is it real?

It is important to understand and define your customer problem carefully,

For example, if you are evaluating selling healthy vegetable juice, the customer problem statement you are trying to address is:

"I want to drink green juice to stay healthy and energetic, but I don't have the time to make it myself"

Let us say you want to build a professional education and training company.

What would your customer's problem statement look like?

"I need to upgrade my skills in order to get promoted in my current job as well as to find new job opportunities"

It is important that the problem you have identified is "real" and is not just something you think might exist. To verify your hypothesis, talk to potential customers and ask them to confirm that they indeed faced the problem.

How would you do that? Not every person walking on the road is your potential customer. You will have to define a target "profile" in order to narrow down who you should reach out to.

Let's say the customer problem you are trying to solve is:

"I am a working woman and I need more choices for high quality western business attire"

Assume you are living in Bangalore, India. In order to test out this hypothesis, your target profile could look something like this:

- Females aged 25-35 years
- Working in IT companies in Mumbai
- Earning high disposable income
- Wear western business attire regularly

Now that you have a profile, start identifying people with this profile. Look at your social circle—friends, colleagues, and acquaintances.

Once you identify these people, talk to them and validate the hypothesis created in your problem statement. Do they face the problem you are trying to solve? If yes, what are the reasons? What motivates them? What is their social and professional behaviour? How do they buy? What do they like and dislike?

For instance, in our clothing line example, understand what motivates your target set of women. What do they expect from western attire? Where do they buy? What do they value? Is it quality, convenience, style, fit, or price?

Do not collect this information via surveys, as people do

not think hard enough while responding. Talk to your target customers face-to-face or over the phone. As you gather more information, keep refining the problem statement—make it precise and be as specific as possible. Fine-tune your product or service to serve these 100 customers in the best possible way.

How is your solution better than competition?

Understand the competition. If your identified problem is real, chances are someone is already solving it.

If you believe there is no competition, either you have not thought hard enough, or researched hard enough . . . or your problem statement is not real.

In all the examples above, we can identify competition:

- <u>Healthy juices:</u> Gym clubs, raw vegetable vendors, roadside juice vendors, packaged juices.
- <u>Professional education:</u> Colleges, certification programs, internal company learning programs, private commercial training companies (some are specialised in computer learning or in leadership training; others are full-service providers).
- <u>Professional attire:</u> Traditional retail stores, online stores, tailors in and around the neighbourhood.

Ground research can go a long way in helping you understand not only the customer problem but also where existing solutions are lacking.

Suhani Mohan (Saral Designs) did significant primary research before jumping on the idea of an affordable high-quality female hygiene product.

"While I was working at Deutsche Bank, I learnt about the deplorable situation of menstrual hygiene in India. Being born and brought up in an urban setting, I did not know what it would take to work towards solving a problem in rural India. To learn more, I took a fifteen-day tour around rural India (Jagriti Yatra), spoke with several women across different states . . .I realised that most of the low cost production units were running into cash flow issues due to insufficient scale and lack of demand for the poor product quality."

As you identify the competition, you will also understand how crowded the market place is, and how can you win in that space. Evaluate your idea to see if it can solve your customer's problem better than the identified competition.

Do not look for marginal improvements over the existing solutions—as the value that customers perceive will be negligible compared to competition, and they won't buy. Look for drastic improvements and a much higher perceived value than current competing products. The more unique you are, the better your chances of winning a profit-making market for your business.

As we discussed in the last chapter, try to be better than your competition in at least one of three ways: better product/ technology, better cost, and better customer experience. Can you delight the customer in a unique and game changing way?

Google was a much better search engine than Yahoo! and other existing engines. Facebook was a much better social networking platform than Myspace and Orkut. The iPhone was a much better smartphone than Nokia and Blackberry phones.

Low cost airlines opened up air travel to many new middle class travellers. Chinese manufacturers cut down production costs to deliver much cheaper products.

Zappos brought in an entirely new and fresh perspective on customer service, which helped it become a leading online shoe vendor, despite the presence of big players like Amazon.

Just because competition exists, it does not mean that you should not pursue your idea. In fact, if you have competition—be happy! It means that there is a market out there for your product. It means you'll have an easier time explaining to people what you offer.

Are your target customers willing to buy? At what price? Is it profitable?

Once you identify your target customers and confirm that there is a real problem that is not sufficiently being addressed by existing solutions, verify if your solution solves the problem.

But wait a minute. You don't have your product ready, yet. How will you verify? This is the biggest hurdle of your idea evaluation.

Get creative to run experiments! In his book, "*The 4-Hour Workweek*", Tim Ferriss calls it "micro-tests".

"Micro testing involves using inexpensive advertisements to test customer response to a product prior to building."

Explaining your idea verbally won't take you far. Most of the customers will not understand the value of any product or service (unless it is very obvious; which is rare!). Try to provide them your prototype product or service, free. The closer it is to the real thing, the better the feedback you will get.

Zappos is a leading online shoe retailer known for its pioneering customer service. It started small. The founder, Nick Swinmurn, ran an experiment. He wanted to prove his hypothesis that customers are ready to buy shoes online. He took pictures of local shoe stores' inventory and posted them online (Reiss, 2011). He received a positive response and he marched ahead. This experiment helped him in multiple ways:

1. It showed the product (a very simple crude one) to the customer, rather than creating a hypothetical scenario and asking customers to "imagine"
2. It put itself in position to interact with real customers and learn about their needs.

Zappos has been immensely successful and Amazon acquired it for a reported $1.2 billion in 2009.

The ultimate feedback is when you ask your customer to take out the wallet and pay for your product. She might say "I love it" as long as the product is free. But the real test comes when you ask her to buy it. How do you test the intent to buy?

Think about building a Minimum Demo-able Product (MDP). An MDP is a product which the customer can see and feel, and make a decision to buy or not to buy. It is not the actual product, so the customer can't use it (if a customer can use it, it is a Minimum Viable Product (MVP)). But customers can easily evaluate whether it will be useful to them, or not.

Brij Bhushan (Magicpin) created his own experiments to verify his hypothesis.

"We wanted to build something that can be big, where internet and technology can be a differentiator. We wanted to avoid operationally intensive e-commerce and other such ideas. The offline retail market in India was thus a very reasonable choice.

However, the harder part was coming up with the product that was different and that has strong engagement inbuilt. We did not want to build another listing platform for SMEs that customers log in to discover. Our hypothesis was that a locality has a unique character—with merchants, people, and places. And the work and home locations are a key part of everyone's identity. Thus, the challenge was to build a product where we have everyone's identity and people associate with it.

How do we get people to create identities on Magicpin? That's where "selfies" came in. Clicking picture of yourself at local outlets (especially food) with your friends and family is a very common activity made even easier by access to smartphones and internet. If we can get people to submit that content, we can solve the problem of identity. We tested this hypothesis by running many experiments on Facebook and WhatsApp. One experimented had 30+ people sharing their moments with us in less than one day. From there on, we knew that we can build something meaningful. Today Magicpin has almost 1M+ content units, we drive more than 100cr+ business towards local outlets, an average user logs in 5 times a day and interacts with people and places around them."

It is easy to run "micro-tests" online. An example could be:

- Set up a simple product website through a standard website creator.
- Tell customers what you are trying to sell; ask them to "pre-order" it at a special discounted price.
- When one clicks on the link to buy, take them to a landing page saying "Please sign up and we will reach out when the product is available."

- Bring traffic to your product website through a small Google or Facebook ad campaign.
- See the conversion rates: How many people visit? How many people click on "buy"?

Remember the most important metric is how many customers click "buy". People might be super interested in your product, only if they get it free. If you do not intend to charge your customers, it is okay. But if you want your customers to pay directly, then make sure you understand "intent to buy", and not just "intent to use".

Through these micro tests, try to get a sense of how much your customers are willing to pay for your product or service. Do a back of the envelope calculation and come up with what it will cost you to offer the product/service. And answer the question: Is this idea profitable?

One final word of caution before we move on. As I mentioned in the first chapter, government regulations and regulatory changes can impact your business in a negative way. When evaluating your business idea, do your due diligence on the industry and its regulatory landscape before going too far.

2. Can you find the cash to start?

Put it simply, there are three major phases for a startup:

1. Build a Minimum Viable Product (MVP)
2. Acquire the first real customer, and
3. Expand/grow the customer base

Estimate your cash requirement to cross each stage.

How much cash do you need to build an MVP? For instance, if you are thinking of a software business, consider:

- Number of people (x salaries)
- Office space
- Equipment (laptops, data centre capacity, machinery, etc.)
- Registration
- Software licences

How much cash do you need to go from MVP to first customer sale? Consider:

- Sales person cost
- Minimum guarantees
- Inventory cost
- Customer support
- Deployment and delivery cost (which you might have to spend upfront for a payment later)
- Payment schedule

How much cash do you need to grow your customer base? Consider:

- Sales cost
- Marketing cost
- All the previous costs, but at a larger scale

Ideally, you should have the cash required to cross the first two stages when you start. It could come from a variety of sources—be it your personal savings (we will talk about it later), funds from friends and family, or even a bank loan or credit line.

When you evaluate a business idea, estimate this cash requirement. Understand if you have access to this cash when you start. If you believe your idea would need a significant cash investment on Day One, but can't raise this amount through known avenues, maybe the idea is not the best one to pursue.

3. Can you find your customers in a sustainable way?

How are you doing so far in evaluating your idea?

We have talked about evaluating whether you can identify 100 real customers and sell profitably to them.

Say you passed this test. Now you will want to expand your reach beyond these first 100 customers.

And finding customers is NOT easy. It is complex and expensive.

In his book, "*The Lean Startup*" Eric Reiss explains it very well. He calls it the "growth engine" of the company (Reiss, 2011). A startup can make money in three ways:

A. Repeat usage: The value of the product is so compelling that the customer sticks to it. Even if there is a new competitor in the market offering something similar at a lower price, the customer does not switch loyalties. Inherently, such products or services should have a repeat usage model.

B. Viral usage: In today's hyperconnected world, if you can get your customers to refer to other potential users (without a high cost to you), you have hit a gold mine. Facebook is a great example of a product that grew virally. Back in 2005, even after its success in the US market, it was not widely used in India. Orkut was the number one social platform. At some point, people started moving to Facebook (and withdrawing from Orkut). Just because your friends were moving to Facebook, you were compelled to move. In a short span of time, Facebook overtook Orkut in India as the leading social platform.

C. Paid engine of growth: Finally, you can spend money to get customers. For this to work, the amount of money you make from a single customer should be greater than what you are spending on acquisition.

While evaluating your business idea, you should look at these factors. Does your business provide real value to the customer? And does it have a sustainable growth engine? If you expect to build a business by raising funding and paying customers to use your service, odds are you not building a great value in the product and you will run out of gas quite quickly.

4. Can you execute?

A business is 10% idea and 90% execution. Without execution, the best of ideas is worth zero.

What do I mean by "execution"? It is "getting things done" so your product is built, sold, and delivered to your customer. Every little thing counts.

But you might ask: "I am just at the idea evaluation stage. How does execution matter?"

You won't know all the details. But it is important to get a feel for it.

Why?

Because entrepreneurs overestimate their ability to execute or underestimate the complexity of execution. Getting things done is harder than we imagine. Do you remember our earlier discussion around the key survival skill for an entrepreneur: Patience?

How do you develop a good enough level of understanding to evaluate?

It helps if you have past experience. You would know exactly what needs to be done.

If you haven't worked in a related field in the past, talk to people who have. Reach out to industry experts to take feedback on their idea. Ask them about execution—how can the product be launched? How to sell it? Which partnerships are required? What is a typical sales cycle? What are the structural problems in the industry?

Once you draw a rough sketch of the execution map, ask yourself three questions: Do you have the skills, the commitment, and the network to make it work?

Do you have the skills to execute?

Any business follows "the Rule of 2": two skill sets that are at the core of its existence.

Examples:

1. Product development and sales
2. Subject matter experience and sales
3. Subject matter expertise and operations

The core skills to run Google can be software product development + hardware infrastructure development.

The core skills to run Flipkart can be software product + back-end operations.

These skill sets change as a company grows—they morph as the company's new needs appear.

Ideally, you must have at least one of the two core skill sets required to start the company. You can add other skills by either choosing a founding partner with the requisite skills required, or by hiring key people who have these skills.

As we will discuss in next chapter, this is one of the most important criteria while selecting your co-founder.

What happens if you believe you have neither of the two core skill sets? In such a case, I would challenge you to go back to the drawing board and re-think.

Do you have the commitment to execute?

Assess what level of commitment is required to execute your concept.

Here, I am not talking about passion and interest in that idea. I am assuming you will take care of those factors when you answer the question: "Why I want to startup."

I am talking about the pure commitment of two things: Time and Energy.

Figure out how much time it will take to execute this idea and build a business. Some businesses, by nature, take time to build (for example education-related startups face this challenge). Other businesses have stronger network effects resulting in a possible explosive growth. A good way to assess this is to look at the growth of comparable companies. Make sure you understand a realistic timeframe to build your business and then commit to it.

Finally, do you have the right level of physical energy to play your role to execute an idea? One can classify any role as "field-heavy" and "office-heavy".

Sales, marketing, and operations are typically "field-heavy" roles, while product development and engineering are typically "office-heavy" roles. These require different levels and types of physical energy. Do you have that level of energy? Are you willing to commit your energy to your business development?

Do you have a network you can access for support?

Do you have relatives or friends in the industry? Do you have a network to support you?

If you want to start a clothing line business, it helps if you know people in the fashion or retail industry.

If you want to enter the healthy juices business, it helps if you know people in the nutrition or food franchise business.

It is good to connect with people in the industry. They can guide you, help you ask the right questions, assist you in getting an important appointment, speed up things, and give you a view of the operational difficulties you are likely to face. Each business has its own character. You can only get to know this once you have been in the business for a while.

5. Does the idea fit with your "Why"?

Earlier in this book, we looked at why you want to start up. We discussed why it is important for aspiring entrepreneurs to have clear reasons for launching a startup. We discussed financial, professional, and personal reasons for starting up.

When you consider an idea, you should ask whether it will help you achieve your goals and aspirations. While the exact outcome is uncertain today, you should beware of signing up for an idea completely at odds with your stated motivations.

If your financial goal is to create a billion-dollar company, then a social NGO might not be the best choice for you.

If your professional goal is to build the next technology product to solve an important problem, then a software services business for SAP might not be the best business for you.

If your personal goal is to lead a good lifestyle with a sustained cash flow, then building a valuation-based social networking company might not be the best business for you.

A simple way to evaluate your idea is to understand whether it is a cash business or an equity business.

If people ask you, "How will you make money?" after hearing your business idea—there is a strong chance it is an equity-focused business. An equity-focused business focuses on creating long-term assets, which you can leverage to generate cash in the distant future.

Those assets can be customer base, a killer product, or a massive distribution system. The business model is fast changing and not proven yet. For a good long time, you will be "burning cash," instead of "earning cash".

VCs and other equity investors will be interested in your business because they can generate a hundred-fold return.

Most of the "next gen" technology companies are equity-based businesses.

On the other hand, cash businesses have a proven business model. Your focus regarding cash is to make sure you have a positive operating cash flow (you are "in the black" as opposed to "in the red") as soon as possible. You won't get a hundred-fold return for yourself or any investor, so a cash business is less attractive for VCs.

Good examples of a cash business are traditional retailers, restaurants, consulting, and law firms. We are surrounded by cash businesses.

You should match your financial, professional, and personal reasons with the type of business you are considering. See whether you have the right fit or not. Here is a way of looking at that:

Reason	Equity	Cash
Financial	Long-term big equity reward; uncertain short term cash	Short-term success at creating a steady cash flow
Professional	Higher risk; higher upside	Lower risk; upside might be limited
Personal	Higher possibility of widespread recognition; bad choice for your lifestyle	Sustainable lifestyle; might not result in a widespread recognition or huge wealth

Table 1: Cash vs. Equity Business

If you feel that the idea will not satisfy your goals, it is a big red flag. However attractive the business potential is, you will end up being dissatisfied.

Recap

We talked about the "Startup Idea Evaluation template".

1. Can you identify and profitably serve 100 customers?
    - Can you define the customer problem? Is it real?
    - How is your solution better than competition?
    - Are your target customers willing to buy? At what price? Is it profitable? Is this price higher than your cost?
2. Can you find the cash to start?
3. Can you acquire customers in a sustainable way?
4. Can you execute, i.e., can you transform the idea into business?
    - Do you have the skills to execute?
    - Do you have the commitment to execute?
    - Do you have resources you can access for support?
5. Does the idea fit with your "Why"? (Cash vs. Equity business)

Try to evaluate one of your many ideas (the best one in your mind), based on the above; and see how it goes.

Send me a message on Twitter @Pango about your experience; I'd love to hear your views on how we can improve this template.

CHAPTER FIVE

Choosing Your Co-founder

"HE IS MY BEST BUDDY,
LET'S START UP WITH HIM."

My second biggest mistake in my entrepreneurial journey was how I chose my co-founder. (Not knowing my "Why" before I started was the first)

My co-founder was my classmate in college. We had been good friends for five years, and I knew him to be intelligent, driven, and dedicated. Our skills were complimentary and splitting responsibilities was easy: I looked after business development and sales, while he was in charge of product development and engineering.

Who could be a better co-founder?

As time progressed, we found we had different motivations to start a business. Our vision for the company was also different. Neither of us was wrong, but we were not aligned. As a result, we could not build a roadmap for the future of our company. We suffered. The company suffered.

The biggest decision of your startup

"Your biggest life decision is who you marry"

"Your biggest startup decision is who your co-founder is"

As an entrepreneur, you should be very thoughtful and conscious while choosing your co-founder. As an angel investor, I come across multiple startups. When I evaluate them, the first criterion—and the most important one—is the founding team. What is the strength of the founding team? Independent of the business idea, will I bet on the co-founders? If the answer is no, I do not evaluate the idea at all. You can change everything in a startup later—the product, services, employees, or even the idea itself—but you cannot change the founding team.

The founding team is the startup.

It is the heart and soul of the company. If the founding team is not strong, the startup is doomed to be a failure.

Paul Graham is a noted Angel investor and venture capitalist, who co-founded the Y Combinator seed capital firm. His essays on startups are worth gold and highly recommended.

In his essay on Angel investing, he lays it out well (Graham, P. (n.d.). http://www.paulgraham.com/angelinvesting.html)

"There is an ongoing debate between investors which is more important, the people, or the idea—or more precisely, the market. Some, like Ron Conway, say it's the people—that the idea will change, but the people are the foundation of the company. Whereas Marc Andreessen says he'd back okay founders in a hot market over great founders in a bad one . . .I think you want to go with Ron Conway and bet on people"

It is astonishing how casually entrepreneurs choose their co-founders, without putting in enough thought and due diligence.

As in my case, as well as for several other entrepreneurs I have spoken with, the choice of a co-founder was not something to which they had given much thought. In most cases, they picked their closest friend. Many of these founding teams were successful in working together to create a new business. Yet, many failed. Some started well, but failed later when the business came to difficult crossroads and they needed to make a do-or-die decision.

> "When you start something, the first and most crucial decision you make is who to start it with. Choosing a co-founder is like getting married, and founder conflict is just as ugly as divorce . . .if the founders develop irreconcilable differences, the company becomes the victim."
>
> Peter Thiel, *Zero to One* (Thiel, 2014).

While Thiel has compared choosing a co-founder to getting married, I love comparing the founding team to a couple deciding to have a child without getting married (or any other social and legal binding). Giving birth to and raising a child is a huge task, which requires a tremendous amount of commitment, passion, and energy. It requires an alignment of two people's goals and priorities in life. A social or a legal contract like marriage helps in the construct because it acts as a binding force between the two parents (at least for some time). Starting a company needs exactly the same level of commitment and alignment, but with no legal or social bind.

Can you just do it alone?

Do you even need a co-founder for your venture?

You can do it alone, but it will be difficult to succeed. Two to three founders are involved in starting most new businesses, and not a single individual. Why?

The first reason is skill sets.

We have discussed "the Rule of 2": two skill sets core to its existence. It can be product development plus sales, subject matter experience plus sales, subject matter expertise plus operations, or any other combination.

Most of us are excellent at one thing, good at two or three things, and average to poor at others. A startup needs excellence. Good or average is just not acceptable.

You, as a founder, might end up harming the company more than helping it if you stretch yourself to new areas. Beware of your ego here! You might puff up and say, "I know all that I need to know!" True? Maybe. Usually not.

The second reason is man-hours.

Let us assume you are a superman with expertise in all the skills required to start a company. Nonetheless, you have one constraint: you can only work twenty-four hours in a day.

Or—you cannot! Because, even Superman needs to sleep!

As a startup, you have to maintain a high standard in product development, sales, or operations. You are a small company and you have to compete hard and excel in all areas to maintain your edge. If you, as sole founder, try to do it all alone, it will take its toll on you personally. At some point, quality—of more than just your product—will start to suffer.

The third reason is psychological.

Launching a startup is a battle. This battle will stress you out. You need a partner in this journey—someone to talk to and discuss the most difficult topics. You need a partner to share the load and to do things that you cannot. You need a co-founder from the very start to sail through the tough waters.

If you are thinking of going alone, think again. Ultimately, you will have to decide, but you should know the risks.

Your best friend or spouse is NOT always the best co-founder!

Has your list of potential co-founders revolved around your five best mates?

You are not alone. This is how most entrepreneurs approach the search for the perfect co-founder.

In reality, professional chemistry can be very different from personal chemistry. You might find a person awesome in a social atmosphere, to accompany on trips, and to have fun with. But working with the same person in a professional environment can be a very different experience.

Similarly, your spouse or favourite family member may not always be your best choice for co-founder. Just because you may know him or her for several years and share a great personal relationship does not mean that you will form a great founding team when you start a company.

It is important to consider the possibility that when something goes wrong with your startup, it may end up negatively impacting your personal relationship as well, resulting in a double whammy. Is that a risk you are willing to take? The stress of failure can be huge and the best of relationships may not be able to withstand the dual impact.

Do not get me wrong—your family/friends might still be the best choice for you. But you must evaluate dispassionately and make a rational, justified, and well-pondered decision.

Can you work together for long hours to develop a product?

Can you agree on a shared vision for a business?

Can you follow a path with all your energy, even if you disagree with it?

Put them under the same rigorous evaluation as you would put any new acquaintance.

Your choice of a co-founder cannot be about making your friend or family member "happy". Do not allow your emotions to control the most important decision for your startup.

What should you look for in a co-founder?

How should you go about choosing your co-founder(s)?

I suggest you consider these four questions:

1. Do they bring skill sets to the table that are complementary to your own?
2. Can you work with them in a professional environment?
3. Are your goals, values and mission aligned with theirs (i.e., Are your motivations aligned)?
4. Do you trust them?

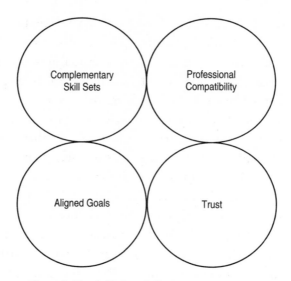

Figure 5: The 4 Circles of Choosing A Co-Founder

1. Complementary skill sets

As an entrepreneur, you have to first identify the most critical skills required to **start** your business. You may need additional skills to scale your business or make it successful, but those can come later.

If you want to build a business around an e-commerce portal, you might need a technology and a retail expert. Thereafter, you can hire people with expertise in supply chain, operations, finance, etc. If you are looking to start a human resources consulting business, one of the co-founders must have the relevant HR background to understand customer requirements deeply and talk the same language.

Does your co-founder have the necessary talents and skills that are different from yours, and just as strongly developed— or more?

Siddhartha Agrawal (Wallsoft Labs) wanted to build an algorithmic trading platform. He needed two skills: an understanding of how the market operated and coding. He knew the market—in and out. He was missing a developer.

"I knew I had to partner with another technologist, more specifically, someone rounded enough to be a great developer but also with a business sense. I was confident that a team of two people had a better chance of surviving than one, so I picked on the best developer I knew and trusted, who was with me during undergrad and Microsoft both."

Suhani Mohan (Saral Designs) was looking at the idea of decentralised production of manufacturing sanitary pads. She found a perfect co-founder in Kartik Mehta. Kartik is an Engineering Design graduate from IIT Madras and had worked on machine design and development for three years with General Motors, and Neubauplan Design Studio. As Kartik was also looking to work on more challenging products that could impact a large number of people, they started Saral Designs in June 2015.

Keeping in mind the "Rule of 2", which are the two skills without which you cannot even start your business? Between your co-founder and you, are you strong on those two skills?

2. Professional Compatibility

Managing a startup is not a sprint, but a marathon. For this marathon, you need a partner whose true character is put to the test. He might be great fun to hang out with, but she should be a great person to work with 24 x 7 x 365 under trying and tiring situations. Learn to differentiate clearly between "I don't like the person" versus "I don't like the way we work together."

Do you like working with this person as a professional?

Do you like their work ethic, problem-solving approach, and attitude?

Do you feel comfortable with how they interact with different types of people (vendors, employees, peers, and customers)?

Do you have any idea how this person holds up under pressure and reacts to tough business situations?

If you have not worked with your prospective co-founder in a professional setting, it can be difficult to assess her professional "personality". Talk to her work colleagues or people who might have worked with her to understand her strengths and weaknesses. Do your due diligence. It is a matter of life and death for the dream of your life!

And lest you think I am being one-sided, let me remind you that your co-founder(s) must also believe that your partnership can work. In other words, they should be doing the same due diligence as you, for your startup to work. Better still, insist on it!

3. Aligned Goals/Motivations

Do you understand your future co-founder's motivations to start a business?

Are those reasons aligned with yours?

Do you understand what type of business he wants to create?

Is it aligned with your vision?

If your co-founder's motivation is not real and strong enough, he might not put in the effort required to succeed and might quit in the middle.

If he wants to run a cash business and you prefer an equity business, it will result in a clash and become difficult to make tough decisions for the company.

Understanding someone else's goals and values is not an easy task. Try to have long conversations with potential co-founders. From your side, over-communicate. Ask ten times; explain ten times. If you cannot decode their mind, speak up and ask direct, pointed, specific questions! It can be hard to have these kind of conversations and easy to escape them with a "We'll figure it out" response; but remember, better identify any red flags now rather than two years out when things get out of control.

4. Trust

All things said and done—you should be able to trust your co-founder. Trust compensates for ambiguity. Everything is not crystal clear from Day One for any company. The roles, responsibilities, authorities, ownership, and power: everything changes very fast. In these dynamic situations, trust will strengthen the building and save it from collapsing.

Do you trust your co-founder with your startup?

Do you trust your co-founder to put in 120% effort?

Do you trust your co-founder to survive through tough times?

Do you trust your co-founder to be transparent in communication?

Brij Bhushan (Magicpin) believes mutual trust and respect are of utmost importance.

"I've known Anshoo, for 8+ years. We worked together at Bain & Co. We were on same projects, stayed in the same place, and car pooled to office. I've always respected and admired him for his work ethic, smartness, and just the deep desire to be the best at whatever he picks up. When Anshoo shared his desire to go on the same path, it was a very easy decision to take. It is important to start with someone whom you trust and respect."

Siddhartha Agrawal (Wallsoft Labs) talks about how trust is important. He talked to his future co-founder about the idea of an algorithmic trading platform. Both were developers at Microsoft; and the distinction of roles and responsibilities was not very clear on Day One. Siddhartha acknowledged this, but continued to move ahead because his co-founder and he trusted each other and believed that they will together make the right decisions for the company.

"We did not have a clear distinction of the roles, because we trusted each other instinctively, having gone back a long way. Anything that was up for decision was mutually discussed and agreed upon. Even today, we trust each other to take the right decision and abide by it even if the other one feels it was incorrect."

Founder "Prenup"

So, you looked long and hard within the intersection of the four circles, and finally found the co-founder of your dreams. Now what? Before you proceed, there are some important points to agree upon with your co-founder(s).

In a Harvard Business Review article titled "The Very First Mistake Most Startup Founders Make" (Noam Wasserman, 2016), the researchers concluded:

". . . even the best of ideas can falter when the founding team neglects to carefully consider early decisions about the team: the relationships, roles, and rewards that will make the founders a winning team . . ."

You need a prenup with your co-founders.

Prenup is short for prenupital agreement—a contract entered into prior to marriage around division of property and support in case of divorce or breakup of marriage.

(https://en.wikipedia.org/wiki/Prenuptial_agreement)

As "conflict-avoiding" humans, co-founders often tend to avoid talking about their inner concerns, such as "What happens if my co-founder leaves within the first six months? Should she get her equity? What will I do if I think she is not contributing enough?" etc. before starting up. A "founder prenup" forces open dialogue between co-founders on these key issues before they start working together, and prevents them from becoming a point of contention later on.

A prenup might seem like an awkward and unnecessary thing to do (especially when you start off with a lot of trust in each other). But it can help bring stability to your startup in the future. It is always more comfortable to talk about conflict when there is none!

Your startup is your dream. You do not want it to suffer because of other co-founders, or even yourself.

In my view, a founder prenup must, at minimum, include these elements.

1. Roles and responsibilities
2. Equity split
3. Vesting schedule and exit clause
4. Intervention mechanism

Let us talk through each one of these in detail. Please note I am providing some guidelines here. These guidelines must be used as a starting point. The exact terms and conditions for your prenup should be customised based on the unique nature and needs of your startup.

1. Roles and responsibilities

A prenup must include clear roles and responsibilities for each co-founder. Titles don't matter as much as clarity around who "owns" what. It will help measure the contribution of each player to the startup when it comes to decisions around equity split.

The key roles in a technology startup, especially in its early stages, are as follows:

Chief Technology Officer (CTO): Who owns the design, development, and delivery of the core offering of a technology startup? Or the IT platform for a tech enabled startup? It includes gathering requirements, creating the prototype, and actual coding (if you are building a software product). As the company matures, there may be the need for a separate Chief Product Officer role that focuses entirely on product development and making the offering useful to your customers.

Chief Sales Officer (CSO): Who owns sales and business development for the product (or service)? Who owns figuring out the right lead generation engine? It includes customer leads, sales process, demos, customer delivery, and customer support.

Chief Financial Officer (CFO): Who owns cash management, accounting, raising funds, and building financial projections for the company? Who interfaces with potential or actual investors?

Team Builder: Who owns building a team beyond the co-founders? If I have to vote for the toughest part of building a startup—I would nominate hiring and retaining people. You need one co-founder to own it end to end. It means understanding whom to hire and when, building a network of potential candidates, "dating" them, talking to recruiters, going through CVs, running the selection process, negotiating with them, etc.

Chief Operations Officer (COO): Who owns getting things done on time? Who owns the overall schedule and timelines for the startup? Who keeps a finger on the pulse of company operations? Who makes sure people get their laptops, bills are paid on time, office space is booked, etc.?

Chief Executive Officer (CEO): Finally, one founder must be the CEO to bring it all together. The CEO is responsible for everything and influences the success or failure of the company. He or she is the primary spokesperson—the face of the company, and plays a key role in fundraising, recruiting for senior roles, and everyday decision making. Typically when starting up, the CEO often wears the multiple hats of CFO, Team Builder and COO, and in some cases, even the CSO!

The choice of a CEO is not an easy one. It is important that co-founders do not decide to be CEO just because they want to attach the title to their name. The CEO must possess skills, such as good communication, selling skills, and a willingness to take hard decisions. All else being equal more experience must be taken into consideration!

2. Equity Split

Many founders end up splitting the company 50:50 to avoid conflict and give a sense of being "fair".

Noam Wasserman, a Harvard Business School professor has spent fifteen years studying high-stakes decisions at more than 6,000 startups. In the Harvard research paper that he authored along with Thomas Hellmann, they studied equity splits adopted by over 3,700 founders from over 1,300 startups in the US and Canada, and concluded that entrepreneurs too often split equity with a "quick handshake." They shared the experience of Robin Chase, the co-founder of Zipcar, a car-sharing company in the US.

Robin wanted to avoid conflict with her co-founder and proposed a 50/50 split in the very first meeting. She was just getting to know the co-founder professionally. Soon, she realised her "quick handshake" was a mistake. While Robin left her job, her co-founder did not, and only contributed marginally. Robin was not happy.

A "fair" split of equity should be a composite of multiple factors: idea, work distribution, cash investment, time commitment, and in some cases, relevant experience.

I propose an "Equity Split Calculator" below. The idea is to come up with a "formula" to arrive at a "fair" split. You may customise the roles and equity percentages here (and add other variables to the mix, for e.g. level of experience) based on the unique business or execution model of your startup; but what is critical here is that the equity split is an outcome of a well thought out deliberation that is agreed to, upfront, by all co-founders, rather than being the result of a split second decision.

Idea	Whose idea was it in the first place?	10%
Who does what?	CTO / CPO	30%
	CSO	20%
	CFO	10%
	Team builder	10%
	COO	10%
	CEO	10%
Who brings in upfront cash?	Upfront cash should be treated as a credit. Founders should be allocated debentures, which can be converted to equity at the time of a formal fundraising round (at a certain discounted rate). I do not support allocating upfront equity based on cash investment.	

What is the level of time commitment?	Sweat equity matters! Part-time founders should be penalised.	**After calculating the equity from above, reduce a part-time co-founder's equity by 50% and re-distribute it to other full time founders**
Cash salary?	If a founder decides not to take cash salary, he/she should be issued an equivalent value of debentures. These debentures may be converted into equity	

Table 2: "Equity Split" Calculator

Here is an example.

Suppose there are three founders—Amar, Akbar, and Anthony.

	Amar	**Akbar**	**Anthony**
Whose idea was it in the first place?	√ (10%)		
CPO/CTO		√ (30%)	
CSO			√ (20%)
CFO	√ (10%)		
Team builder	√ (10%)		
COO	√ (10%)		
CEO	√ (10%)		
Total	50%	30%	20%
Who works part-time?	Full time	Full time	Part-time
Reduce equity of Part-timer			(50% of 20%) = 10%
Equity to be redistributed	+5%	+5%	-10%
Final total	55%	35%	10%

Table 3: Example of "Equity Split" Calculator

3. Vesting schedule and Exit clauses

Equity should be vested over a period of four years.

In year one, vest a smaller number. Typically, founders are committed to staying on for one year.

In year two, have a bigger amount vested. The time between year one and year two is usually the most critical in ramping up the business. A good distribution, year-wise, from year one to year four might be 10/40/30/20.

Finally, what happens when a co-founder exits the company?

Include an exit clause in your partnership agreement. It should state how the equity is vested, redistributed, or sold; what to do with debt and all types of legalities of separation. Put it on paper, in writing. It goes without saying that you should get an attorney's help.

4. "Intervention" mechanism

We all know the startup ride will invariably be bumpy. Disagreements will occur between founders and tension will crop up. This is normal and expected.

Most of the time, you will resolve such disputes. But sometimes, there may be "fundamental" disagreements. What if you feel a founder is not working hard enough or not making enough progress? What if you do not agree with the current direction in which the product is going? What if founders have a disagreement on the vision for the company?

Such big disconnects within the founding team need to be resolved quickly. I recommend founders set up an "Intervention" mechanism upfront to handle such situations.

What can be some intervention mechanisms?

- Founders meet in their favourite place to discuss in an informal setting, exchange barbs, and finally one person decides.
- Founders discuss the topic in the presence of a common mentor/arbitrator, whose advice they take and decide.
- Founders have a quick one-on-one discussion.

By setting up this mechanism, founders won't have to think about "How to raise the issue?" "Should I talk to the òther person directly?", "Will I be seen as a trouble maker?", "Maybe I should wait for some time" and so on. It eliminates anxiety and complexity.

A founder prenup agreement may sound crazy, but it will make things easier in the long-run. Try it out!

What if you can't find a co-founder?

If you can't find a co-founder—that special person with just the right skills to complement your own—what should you do?

My advice is—don't stop, don't wait. The startup is all about you and your dreams. If you are unable to find a co-founder, hire people and get started. Don't make it an excuse to not get into action.

People start joining once things get started and see <u>tangible</u> results shaping up. It will be easier to convince people to join you once they see your own commitment and passion for your dream-project.

Recap

Let's summarise.

- The founding team makes or breaks a startup. Think about your co-founder carefully.
- It is difficult to start a company on your own.
- Your best friend or spouse might not be the best choice as co-founder.
- In a co-founder, consider: "Does this person have a skill set which I don't have?", "Can I work with this

person in a professional set up (not personal)?", "Are this person's motivations aligned with mine, and do we share the same vision for the company?" and, finally, "Can I trust this person?"

- Sign a "Founder Prenup" which lays out clear roles, equity split, vesting and exit clause, and intervention mechanisms.

  - There are six roles in a startup: Product, Sales, Cash, Building team, Operations, and CEO. Decide who does what and who is who, upfront.

  - 50/50 split is not a "fair split." Use the "Equity Split calculator" to calculate a "fair split" of equity based on actual contribution. Have a vesting schedule.

- Finally, if you don't find a co-founder, don't wait too long. It is your dream, it is your journey. Get started and people will join you.

Finally . . .

"Wannabe" entrepreneur in school or college: Is your best buddy your co-founder? Fair enough. Have you worked together? If no, find a way to work together before you start up. Maybe a course or a small assignment?

"Friday-night-after-two-drinks" reluctant entrepreneur in your 20s/30s: Your drinking buddies might not be the best co-founders. If you are serious, start looking elsewhere.

"Ready to go" soon-to-be entrepreneur: Do you have a co-founder? If yes, think about the Founder "Prenup". It will bring up the right issues for a discussion.

"Already on the train, but less than 12 months" entrepreneur: How is it going with your co-founder? It might not be too late to consider a "Prenup" agreement with him/her. Consider it.

A real/aspiring VC/Angel investor who has never built a business: For you, the founding team matters a lot. In addition to their personal qualifications and skills, try to assess their mutual compatibility. Are their motivations and visions aligned? Is there open and transparent communication? Do you think their "marriage" will last long? The strength of their relationship might be a good indicator of future success.

CHAPTER SIX

The Final Leg

"I CAN START TOMORROW!"

Y
ou are serious about starting up. You have been validating an idea for a while now. You are getting ready to cut the cord. But before you do that, there are a few additional actions you must consider.

1. Set a timeframe
2. Set up milestones
3. Steel your mind
4. Enlist the support of family and close friends
5. Get your finances in order
6. Upgrade your skills
7. Find a mentor

1. Set a timeframe

A good gambler knows when to fold.

A good trader knows when to sell.

A good entrepreneur knows when to exit.

How much time do you give yourself before you decide to "exit"? Will you decide while on your journey, based on how it's going and how much mental and financial strength you have left at that point? Bad idea as you might never "exit". People don't get the concept of "sunk cost" easily!

I suggest you take control over your future and fix a timeframe for your entrepreneurial journey even before you start. Set a mental alarm for a predetermined time period—say for instance, two years. Before this alarm goes off, keep going, no matter how hard the journey is. After this alarm rings, quit if things do not go as planned.

Why is this important? There are two reasons.

First, you will not consider quitting too early, that is, without giving yourself a fair chance for success. Second, you will not delay the inevitable and cut your losses if things do not go as expected by forcing yourself to quit.

When Mohan Rajagopalan (Yaap.io) was about to leave McKinsey and start up full time, he explained his philosophy to me:

"The framework I used, and the one I recommend is: There are two measurable limits: time and money. Put aside a fixed amount of money. This is your Bank, assuming you get no outside investments this is the amount of money you can afford to burn. Next, set a time limit—this is a hard limit for you to evaluate a Go/No Go!

With these constraints defined, be willing to go all the way—this is a game that ends until either one of the measurable limits is reached. Come up with a realistic set of milestones that you'd like to accomplish, and every three or four weeks track progress. Don't stop short until you reach a limit."

Srikrishnan Ganesan (Konotor) felt the same when he set his timeframe as one year.

"I got into this with a one-year time horizon to see how things work out and always knew getting back into a job wasn't going to be a problem. Had great support from the family. In fact, I never looked at it as a risk–rather as one year of salary I am forgoing, to give a shot at building a product I believe in. The downside of doing a startup was pretty low to me personally (when you think long term)."

Deciding on a timeframe frees up your mind, reduces the variability, and gives you more control. Your choices become simpler, from how much you will need in savings, to what career and financial risk you are taking, to what expectations to set with your family.

2. Set up milestones

Once you have determined a timeframe, you can easily track progress if you create a realistic timeline with actionable milestones.

But how can you create a set of milestones with limited information, when you haven't even started the business? You don't know how customers will react to your product, you don't know how your revenues will ramp up, you don't know when you might need funding, and many such unanswered questions.

In a previous chapter, we talked about how, in a startup, very few things are under your control, while most others are not. My suggestion here is to create a timeline around what you can control more than others.

A simple first pass at a timeline could look like this:

1. Create first prototype within three months
2. Show first prototype to 100 customers within 6 months.
3. Show second version to customers within 1 year.

Why does this make sense? Because you can better control the pace at which you develop your products. You can better control the number of customers you talk to. You can better control the speed at which you will incorporate their feedback and launch the next version.

What will likely not work? A timeline like:

1. Sign up the first customer within six months.
2. Become cash positive within one year.

You do not control the number of customers who sign up. There can be so many uncertainties you have no inkling about, at this point. You have little control over when your company first turns cash positive. At least, not at this stage. Once you jump in, you will know better.

3. Steel your mind

In the first chapter, we talked about all the things that could go wrong. So how can you stop worrying and start doing? How can you steel your mind, so that you are (somewhat) immune to the troughs along your entrepreneurial journey?

Follow these steps:

1. Visualise the worst situation you could be in, if you started up.
2. Make peace with it. Prepare your mind for this worst case and determine a contingency plan if necessary.
3. Now get started on any action you can take so you end up better than this worst case scenario.

Step 1: Visualise the worst situation you could be in, if you started up

If you assume the worst and start with the lowest expectations, you will find that anything that ultimately happens is typically better than expected, leading you to be happy about what has happened, rather than be shocked or depressed. Also, you will be better equipped to deal with the situation, since you have used your time coming up with a plan of action, rather than whiling it away in anxiety or stress.

Kunal Gandhi (LogicRoots) applied this principle when he was thinking about his career, in case he failed at the startup.

"For career, I convinced myself by thinking about the worst case scenario. All my past work—IIT, IIM, and McKinsey— were my cushion. I thought in case I have to go back to corporate, I can find something easily. Maybe at 50% the salary of my peers, but even then it won't be too bad."

It is a strange but powerful principle. When applied in daily life, it can yield amazing results. The fear goes away and you feel a newfound sense of control over the situation.

If you are running to catch a flight or a connection, assume you will miss it. Get over the initial disappointment. Start planning what you will need to do next or what options you have.

If you are waiting for your performance review, assume the worst outcome. It might be an average rating and that's okay. Start thinking about what your next steps need to be. No need to kill yourself with anxiety for a week.

Let us try and apply this principle to starting up.

Your product or service might have no takers. You run marketing campaigns, but receive little traction. Your customer acquisition cost is high and you lose money on every customer. You try many changes to the product, but it does not pick up traction. You are about to run out of cash soon.

While you are trying to fix your startup, your personal life becomes nonexistent. You start working longer and longer hours. You start working on weekends. You cannot spend enough time with your family. You start missing your kid's functions, family vacations, and parties with your friends. You start running out of cash for personal expenses. Your family starts to get worried about you.

You do not have time to exercise or relax. You start eating junk food. You start to gain weight and feel low on energy. Your health begins to suffer.

At the end of your decided timeframe, you are nowhere close to where you wanted to be. You decide to go back to a regular job. You reach out to recruiters and companies. All of them ask about the "gap in employment". You get offers for a lower position with a lower salary than what you were drawing before you started up.

Things can go bad!

Step 2: Make peace with it. Prepare your mind for this worst case and determine a contingency plan if necessary

Let's start with your career. So you might take two steps backward in your career by starting up. But you can likely still land a job that pays you enough to lead a comfortable life. A backup option could be to come back to your current job and position (which you hold before starting up).It means you must leave on good terms and stay connected to your current employer throughout your startup journey.

If you lose all your personal savings—you still have twenty to thirty years of your career left to build your savings.

You can gain back your personal lifestyle balance and health if you follow a disciplined approach to nutrition and exercise.

You will realise that it is not the end of the world if you fail as an entrepreneur. You can recover from most setbacks— except those that are permanent. Your relationships with loved ones, your own mental balance, and your self-confidence—you have to protect these aspects of your life. Everything else, you can get back.

Step 3: Now get started on any action you can take so you end up better than this worst case scenario

Start preparing to improve your chances to succeed. Follow the guidelines in this book to minimise your risks and maximise your chances of success.

In his best-seller "*The 4-Hour Workweek*," Tim Ferriss writes about his philosophy of life (Ferriss, 2009).

"I realised that on a scale of 1-10, 1 being nothing and 10 being permanently life-changing, my so-called worst case scenario might have a temporary impact of 3 or 4. I believe this is true of most people . . .On the other hand, if I realised my best-case scenario, or even a probable-case scenario, it would easily have a permanent 9 or 10 positive life-changing effect . . .There was practically no risk, only huge life changing upside potential"

4. Enlist the support of family and close friends

Most of us are influenced by the people around us. We cannot help but pay attention to what others are saying about us or what others are thinking about us, especially our close ones— our parents, spouse, and friends.

There is nothing to gain by ignoring them. The startup life is tough, and you will need them as your loudest supporters and cheerleaders. You will need them to help maintain your emotional sanity. If you lose their support, life could become tough.

The most important people to talk to, before you startup, are your spouse and your parents.

Do not commit to a startup unless your spouse is on board. You need his or her support, even if it is reluctant or conditional. If you do not have this support, your mental energy and focus will never be on your startup. What is the purpose of chasing your dreams if your spouse is not part of it?

Communicate with him or her clearly and well in advance. Evaluate your business idea together. Discuss the new financial situation and the resulting impact on your lives. Talk about how your daily family life might change once you start your own business. This includes different aspects of life, such as:

- Your working hours
- Your financial income
- The family budget
- Your weekend schedule
- People you will work with
- Your ability and willingness to meet family milestones (e.g. kids)

The more transparent you are upfront, the easier it will be later.

With parents, it is important to educate them on what you are going to do. Many parents do not understand what their kids do, but they are fine with it as long as they are earning a regular paycheck. Now that you are starting a new journey, it is better to explain to them (in simple language), what you are setting off to do.

This will help your parents in two ways:

1. It will help them get comfortable with your business idea, and
2. It will give them the confidence to talk about your business/plans with their friends and relatives! Trust me, it is an important dimension of your parents' lives. Parents love to talk about their kids! (As an added benefit, you can escape from the scene and avoid answering the typical "*kya chal raha hai beta!*" or "what's up these days, son", when well-meaning relatives walk your way)

Your parents might not fully agree with your move. They might hesitantly agree, because they trust and love you. They might warn you and guide you. But you need them to be involved in your startup journey.

Have an honest conversation about your worst-case scenario with them. Prepare them for this situation. Let them know your contingency plan in case this worst case happens. It will reassure them that your life will still go on, even if you fail miserably.

Kunal Gandhi (LogicRoots) talked to his parents early enough.

"I had a good chat with my parents. They are smarter than me. They were never convinced, but finally gave strong support. It is important to communicate early."

Srikrishnan Ganesan (Konotor) got instant strong support from his family.

"My dad always wanted me to start up. I didn't have huge commitments of my own. So it wasn't hard. There were doubts from time to time when things weren't going great and my folks did wonder how long I would persist and ask me if all is fine once in a while. I think they were more worried when they saw me worried or stressed at times."

Suhani Mohan (Saral Designs) followed a brilliant approach. She went a step ahead, presented her idea to her parents, and convinced them fully.

"Earlier my parents were apprehensive about my leaving a coveted job for something unknown, but then I gave them a proper pitch, took all their questions on the risks, the future plans etc. After that day, they have given their unconditional support to me for my decision and my venture. I felt it was very important to convince my parents, since they have known me for the longest time and trust me, if I am unable to convince them, then I will also not be able to convince co-founders, new recruits, customers, or investors either."

5. Get your finances in order

If you start up, you will likely forego a regular income for some time. It can put severe pressure on your personal financial situation. I strongly recommend having a plan in place before you start, so that you and your family do not go through financial distress.

Founders take different approaches to this.

Chaya Jadhav (VirtualMob) said,

"My partner was very supportive and I didn't have to worry on the financial end, not a lot in the beginning at least. I knew if things don't work out, I can go back to work and gave it 6 months to try things out. And we were lucky to get it going."

Siddhartha Agrawal (Wallsoft Labs) shared:

"All my family members were earning well so there were no dependents. My wife was earning significantly so we had a comfortable runway of about a year before we would face financial problems."

Suhani Mohan (Saral Designs) had worked for two and a half years at an investment bank and was very frugal in general, which helped her manage her personal finances easily.

For Divakar Sankhla (Alohomara), having his wife working and supporting the family finances gave him the much-needed extra cushion.

Akshat Choudhary (BlogVault and ActivMob) worked out a formula similar to mine—lead a simple life, cut down your expenses, and save enough.

To plan your finances, you should estimate the total cash required for the planned timeframe of your entrepreneurial journey by following the three steps outlined below.

Step 1: Estimate your required expenses

Review your last twelve months' personal expenses. Assess how much you spent in different categories.

Now, you may plan to cut down on your expenses when you start up—by leading a simpler life.

Plan for the worst case scenario and assume you will continue to incur all your current expenses throughout the timeframe you have set up for yourself. Add an extra 25% to account for emergencies. This will give you your total cash expenses for the period.

Friendly advice: Don't buy a house

Buying a house means a huge monthly pay out.

If you are renting, you can reduce or increase your rent expense by changing house. If you buy a house, you are stuck.

Buying a house also limits your ability to move cities, or places within a city.

It is an illiquid asset, not easy to sell if you have to. You may be better off with more liquid investments.

I personally believe the real estate market is modern day slavery. Once you buy a house, you are slave to a monthly paycheck. Only a job can offer it. If you are planning to start up, postpone buying a house for as long as you can.

Step 2: Calculate your income

Understand your family income (in hand) through your predetermined timeframe. As we discussed before, consider the worst scenario, which might be that you will not earn a single penny throughout this period. Your spouse might continue to work and earn a paycheck, which is wonderful news. Also take into account any other income generating assets you may have.

Friendly advice: Don't quit your job until you have to

Many entrepreneurs I have talked to believe startup commitment is "100% or nothing".

Mohan Rajagopalan (Yaap.io) was very clear in his approach.

"McKinsey gives you search time to look for jobs etc. I used all of it to work on Yaap and flesh out the idea, funding etc. Some of my mentors did advise consider doing it part-time first. But it was a very binary transition for me . . .now, or never."

Chaya Jadhav (VirtualMob) is another believer in the "100%" camp.

"I was fulltime from day one, there was no cutting cord stage in my life. Running a company is a fulltime job, and in my opinion cannot be done with 50% in!"

I believed the same. Whenever well intentioned friends and family members asked, "Why don't you do it part time?" I would snap back with "What do you mean? A startup requires complete commitment. Doing it part-time does not make sense." It was always zero or one for me.

Over the years, though, I have realised this approach may not always make sense. Why should you take all the risks upfront without any validation of the idea? Why should you stop your regular paycheck, put so much pressure on yourself, put your family's sustainability at risk, and jump into the startup world?

My advice: keep the monthly paychecks coming in for as long as you can. You might feel you need to be 100% committed. Absolutely—I agree. But there is a lot of pre-startup work to be done before you can jump in full time. Try to validate your idea as a side project. Many successful entrepreneurs have done it.

Sabeer Bhatia and Jack Smith, Co-founders of Hotmail, created a business plan for a simple-to-install database. They did not quit their jobs right away. Instead, they spent weekends and evenings to build the product. Later this product morphed into Hotmail (Livingston, 2007).

Step 3: Calculate how much you will need in savings

Evaluate if your family income exceeds your required expenses. If not, how much does it fall short? Any gap will need to be filled through your personal savings.

Friendly advice: Do not include startup **cash requirements in your savings calculation**

As discussed in a previous chapter, when you start up, you will need money in hand on Day One to invest on creating the Minimum Viable Product as well as to acquire your first customer. An ideal plan would be to have this money available in your bank, so you do not need to rely on external funding to set up your venture. However I suggest you not to use your personal savings towards your startup, until you have already accounted for your personal expenses.

You cannot build a startup on an empty stomach. Your personal money is first and foremost for yourself and your family. Based on your savings, you have a "survival time window". Do not shrink the window by investing more of your personal money into your venture. You might kill your venture by taking on too much personal risk.

If your personal money, after accounting for your personal expenses, is insufficient for your startup needs, you can reach out to friends and family, angels, banks, incubators, or venture capital firms. I will not go into more detail here on funding, as there are resources available about how to raise money from these sources outlining the benefits and risks of each.

Do you have enough savings? Consider only liquid assets. Do not include illiquid assets such as real estate. If you answered yes, good—you are ready to go. If you answered no, wait until you can save enough.

You will probably argue with me here with, "I don't have enough cash now, and it will take me another five years to save enough. I can't lose this time, I have to start now." Well, fair enough. You have a point. But are you willing to bet your family's livelihood for your startup? That's the tough question for you and your family.

Friendly advice: If savings are limited, work on generating cash quickly through your startup

You might be in a situation when you do not have the savings to sustain your family for a long time. You have a much shorter runway. You will need to generate additional cash quickly.

You can generate cash when your business itself is cash flow positive. In this case, build a cash focused business, rather than a long-term no-cash equity play.

You will also likely need to withdraw a salary soon—so set the right expectations with co-founders and investors.

I know of some founders continuing to do part-time "consulting" projects to generate cash to fund their personal expenses. You could also consider this approach.

Friendly advice: Reduce exposure to riskier assets

Consider your life as a portfolio. You are making a very risky move—starting up a business. Compensate by de-risking the rest of your life. In other words, your financial portfolio should reflect the increased risk profile of your life.

Minimise your exposure to riskier assets such as equity markets. The last thing you want is news of the stock markets crashing and your savings melting away, in a situation when your business is yet to generate income! Consider lower risk (and hence lower returns) financial assets such as fixed deposits.

6. Upgrade your skills

Before you start up, invest in acquiring any missing skill sets required to run a startup.

If you are into technology, keep up with the latest trends. If you do not have an MBA, learn about management principles. If you don't understand cash management, take a course on accounting. Get to know the basics about debit and credit, payables and receivables, payment terms, Profit & Loss statements, cash flow statements, etc. You can take these courses online or through university programs, as they will be invaluable in making the right decisions when you run your startup.

7. Find a Mentor

Most founders are inexperienced at starting a business. Having a mentor with the right skills and knowledge (ideally one with a startup background), allows you to tap into the experience of someone who has been there and done that.

Often mentors can open doors for you through their own network and connections in the industry. The can provide valuable feedback on your product or service, investor pitches and so on. They can challenge you or offer new ways of thinking. If nothing else, they can serve as a sounding board, provide emotional support and listen without judgement when you are facing a crisis.

Recap

Entrepreneurship can be tough on your personal life. To prepare and minimise the risk, you should consider:

1. Set a timeframe on when you will say "I quit" if things don't work out as expected
2. Setup milestones to track your progress
3. Steel your mind to prepare yourself for the worst case scenario for your business, career, and lifestyle
4. Enlist the support of family and close friends: Open communication helps to set right expectations and get support
5. Get your finances in order as "empty stomach" doesn't build a business
6. Upgrade your skills to be ready for the startup
7. Find a mentor to get guidance and a "sounding board"

CHAPTER SEVEN

Cut the Cord!

"AM I READY NOW?"

We have come a long way.

We started by laying out the business and personal risks you may face as an entrepreneur in the first chapter. In every chapter thereafter, we discussed how to prepare for these risks to increase your chances of success when you start up.

Let's take some time to recap and to evaluate your readiness to take the plunge.

Recap: Preparing to overcome business risks

Let's remind ourselves of the reasons we discussed in the first chapter, as to why a startup might fail:

1. Your product is the problem
2. Your competition kills you
3. The legal system kills you
4. You run out of cash
5. Your team is weak

If you put in the hard work to evaluate the business idea before starting up, I believe you can minimise most of these risks.

For instance, answering the question "Can you identify and profitably serve 100 customers?" will ensure you have adequately considered the product features customers value, what competition you will face and how to address it, as well as what legal hurdles you might face and how to avoid them.

If you ensure that before you start, you have a positive response to "Do you have the cash to start" and "Can you acquire customers in a sustainable way", and you can couple it with good execution ("Can you execute?") including good cash management, you should not be running out of cash anytime soon.

Finally, your founding team will rarely become a cause for concern, if you have thought long and hard about your choice of co-founders—whether they bring the right skill sets to the table, whether they can work well with you, whether their goals and mission are aligned to yours, and if there is trust within the team.

Recap: Preparing to overcome personal challenges

Do you remember what we talked about in relation to the massive personal challenges you will face as a startup founder?

1. Your bank balance will make you cringe
2. Your lifestyle will go for a toss
3. Your personal and social commitments will take a backseat

4. You will always be stressed, in some cases depressed
5. Your family will worry. Sharmaji's son will continue to torture you.
6. Your career will take a hit

The single most effective armour in this battle is your "Why". If you are clear about your "why", it will give you the strength to move forward in your venture despite these challenges. For instance, your bank balance may not be what it could be if you continue to work (in the short term), but your longer term "mission" means much more to you than shorter term financial gains.

We also discussed additional ways to address these personal challenges in the previous chapter ("The Final Leg").

For example, setting a timeframe and controllable milestones for your journey can help limit your "downside".

If you get your personal finances in order before you start and clearly understand how much you have, and plan for how much you will need, you may not need to compromise on your lifestyle after starting up.

If you make peace with the worst case scenario with regards to your post-startup business, career, and lifestyle, and think about what you will do to cope and recover even before starting up, it will take plenty of stress out of the equation.

Open communication with your spouse and family about your plans and preparation will help them understand your journey and celebrate it, instead of worrying.

Finally, upgrading your skills and finding a mentor will help not only with your startup journey, but also to stay relevant in the professional world.

The Final Checklist

Now let's look at a checklist to evaluate your readiness to cut the cord.

Below is a list of simple questions with mostly yes/no answers, which touches upon topics that we have covered in this book.

Think about each question carefully, and answer it honestly, There is no right or wrong answer here, though every "No" response should serve as a reminder that you may have missed something worth considering in your preparation towards starting up.

Remember you are doing it for yourself, not for anyone else. Be transparent with yourself. Set aside your ego. Do not over- or underestimate your preparation.

Do you fully understand the personal and professional "downside" of starting up?	Yes/No
Are you clear on why you want to start up? Can you describe your "why" (goals)? (Answer can't be: I hate my job, I hate my boss, Everybody is doing it these days)	1. I want to solve this problem . . .; OR 2. I want autonomy to control my destiny because . . . ; OR 3. I want to become rich 4. I want to be recognised 5. Something else?
Are you clear on the problem you will solve through your startup?	Give details

Have you identified 100 customers that you can profitably sell to?	Who are they? Give details.
How much cash do you need to start selling?	Explain the math.
Do you know how to generate this cash?	List your sources and timeline.
Can your customers find you in a sustainable way?	How?
Do you know what it will take to execute?	List out skills required to succeed. Rate yourself on these skills.
Will your idea help you achieve your goals?	How?
Do you have a founding team?	Yes/No (If you are going alone, list the reasons here)
Does your team have the necessary skills and knowledge to execute?	List the skills required for your startup and who has these skills
Do your co-founders share your vision and motivation?	Explain the common vision. Put it on paper. Make sure your co-founders agree to it.
Can you work well together?	List the data points which support your answer.
Is there mutual trust within the team?	List the data points which support your answer.

Have you agreed on roles, responsibilities, equity split, and other clauses?	Explain the details
How much time have you given yourself to try?	6 months/1 year/2 years/3 years
What milestones are you realistically shooting for?	List the milestones for the next 30/60/90 days, 6 months, and 1 year
Do you have enough savings to sustain yourself and family for this time?	Explain the math
Have you envisioned your worst case scenario?	Write it down in as much detail as possible.
Have you shared this with your family? If yes, what is their reaction? Do they support you? • Spouse • Parents • Close family members • Close friends	Open communication helps.
What will you do professionally in case you fail? How much will you be able to earn?	Paint different options. Verify the options with your friends and mentors
Do you have a mentor?	How do you engage with him?

Table 4: "Cut The Cord" Checklist

You have likely not thought of everything on this list. And that's okay. There will be many uncertainties. You will figure out things as you go along. Your assumptions might prove to be right or wrong. You will learn and evolve.

Remember that the "known something" is better than "unknown everything."

Taking the plunge

"For all the important things, timing always sucks. Waiting for a good time to quit your job? The stars will never align and the traffic lights of life will never be green at the same time . . . "Someday" is a disease which will take your dreams to the grave with you . . ." (Ferriss, 2009)

Tim Ferriss, in *"The 4-hour Work Week"*

So you want to start up. You know what it means. And you are prepared.

Yet, you hesitate.

You face many doubts and questions. Despite your preparation, your mind makes excuses, such as:

- "I don't know if my idea will work at all! What if it fails?"
- "I don't think I am cut out to be an entrepreneur."
- "I just can't find the time."

Sometimes, all that is left to do is to take the plunge. And to take the plunge, you have to **believe**: In yourself, and in your idea.

At the end of the day, preparation can only get you so far. Despite all the validations, the idea won't be tested fully until you start selling the product to customers. You should have confidence in your business idea, so you can motivate yourself and your team. If you have doubts, you can be sure that your team will have even more doubts.

Suhani Mohan (Saral Designs) shares:

"Between deciding to start up and leaving my job, there was a time that I used to get nightmares that I have run out of all the money. But as soon as I left my job, the fear disappeared. Sometimes it is important to just take the plunge."

Brij Bhushan (Magicpin) advises against getting into analysis paralysis:

"It is important to do research and experimentation before picking the idea, but don't overdo it. Intuition and gut has a big role to play! Trust your judgement and take the plunge. Many people over analyze and never get around to starting up!"

Finally, ask yourself, if several years later, **will you regret not having tried**?

When Amazon's founder, Jeff Bezos was considering leaving his well-paying job to start Amazon, he had a choice to make.

"The framework I found, which made the decision incredibly easy, was what I called—which only a nerd would call—a "regret minimisation framework." So, I wanted to project myself forward to age 80 and say, "Okay, now I'm looking back on my life. I want to have minimised the number of regrets I have." I knew that when I was 80 . . .I was not going to regret trying to participate in this thing called the Internet that I thought was going to be a big deal. I knew that if I failed I wouldn't regret that, but I knew the one thing I might regret is not ever having tried. I knew that that would haunt me every day, and so, when I thought about it that way it was an incredibly easy decision."

Taking the plunge can be difficult. But regret can be worse.

Bronnie Ware is an Australian nurse who spent several years working in palliative care, caring for patients in the last twelve weeks of their lives. She revealed the most common regrets of her patients in the best-selling book *"The Top Five Regrets of the Dying—A Life Transformed by the Dearly Departing"* (Ware).

Here were the regrets, starting at #2:

2. I wish I didn't work so hard.
3. I wish I'd had the courage to express my feelings.
4. I wish I had stayed in touch with my friends.
5. I wish that I had let myself be happier.

And the most common biggest regret?

"I wish I'd had the courage to live a life true to myself, not the life others expected of me."

My dear Reader, live a life that is true to yourself. Don't have regrets!

Believe in yourself and in your idea. Understand what you're up against, prepare yourself, and take the plunge! Start up and turn your dreams into reality!

I wish you good luck. May the force be with you.

After You Start: Five Priorities for the First Twelve Months

"THE JOURNEY HAS BEGUN!"

I f you have already begun your startup journey, first and foremost, congratulations! You had the courage to make one of the biggest and the most difficult decisions of your life. You took the big leap!

How does it feel?

I will leave you with some thoughts on five areas that you can focus on, in the first twelve months: time, product/service, team, cash, and your own self.

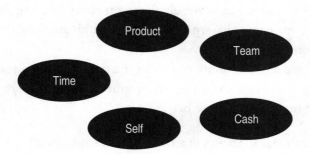

Figure 6: Five Priorities of A Startup Founder

1. Time

Imagine you are in a car going down the slope towards the edge of a cliff. You have to plan and execute your escape. Each second you lose, you are inching closer to death . . .

That's what starting up can feel like.

Time is an extremely critical resource when it comes to entrepreneurship. With every passing day, the opportunity cost of foregoing a steady income increases. As a result, entrepreneurs often feel a constant pressure to make the most of every minute they have available.

Brij Bhushan (Magicpin) shares:

"You always feel that you are not being fast enough. There is always something that can be done better, can be done faster."

It can also go the opposite way. Suddenly you control your own time without any external control factors such as your boss, or your college. Result: Entrepreneurs become lazy or inefficient, especially when faced with ambiguity or difficult decisions.

While it is important not to let the pressure get to you, it is equally important to manage your time wisely. Here are some tips to manage your time better.

A. Don't slack off – A startup is not a sabbatical!

Imagine this scenario:

You start up. On Day One, the regular 6:00 a.m. alarm wakes you up.

You get out of bed, but then realise "Why do I need to wake up at 6? I don't need to start work until 9:00 a.m.!" You feel happy about the newly found freedom. You go back to sleep.

You get up two hours later. But still you are in no hurry. You decide to read the newspaper, lounging on your couch, and sipping a hot cut of tea. Ah! This is the lifestyle and you love it. After all, you wanted to start up for this flexibility!

You finally start working at around 11:00 a.m. You read some emails, waste time on Facebook—it is 2:00 p.m. already. Suddenly, you come across an article on "Game of Thrones". Oh no! You completely forgot about catching up with your favourite TV show. You start streaming it immediately. You know you should get back to work, but—hey—there is lots of time left in the day!

It is 5:00 p.m. now. You always wanted to take a leisurely stroll in the park nearby, but never reached home early enough from work to do it. Well, you can do it now.

You follow it up with a long, relaxed dinner. It is 10:00 p.m. already—not much work done today. But you are happy. You have so much time in your life now. You needed the time to unwind!

In the following days, you experience several more days where you continue to "unwind".

If this has happened to you, I don't blame you. Perhaps for the first time in your life, you are feeling a sense of real freedom. In the past, you always experienced external control: whether it was school timings, college classes, or at work. Now you are the master of your time. You don't know how to live such a life.

Beware of this mind set. You have to be at the highest level of efficiency and productivity. Do not treat startup as a sabbatical!

Treat time as a limited pool of cash. Each second you waste, you are depleting that pool of cash. At some point, you will run out. You need to make progress each day to win more cash, to win more time to survive.

Get things done. Push and move ahead. Become a ruthless action machine!

B. Prepare a plan

In a previous chapter we talked about setting up "controllable" milestones before you begin your journey. You need a plan to achieve these milestones. Create a detailed project plan, broken down into tasks and activities with realistic timelines. Track it periodically, rate your progress against this plan.

C. Follow a schedule

A daily, weekly, and monthly routine, with clearly defined slots for work and leisure can provide you with stability and rhythm.

Maintain your calendar and follow it strictly.

Find time to exercise and relax. It is crucial to maintain the balance. Remember to "calendar" the time to exercise!

D. Plan your next day the previous night

The first few hours of the day are usually the most productive. If you already know what needs to be done, you can get started early, instead of wasting time on thinking about what to do.

E. Set tight deadlines

Parkinson's law (https://en.wikipedia.org/wiki/Parkinson% 27s_law) dictates that work expands to fill the time available for its completion.

If I give you twenty-four hours to complete a job, you will finish it in 24 hours with decent quality. If I give you a week, you will likely "plan" for six days and still finish the job in the last twenty-four hours.

Set up your deadlines accordingly. There is little marginal benefit in working on a problem for long periods of time. Instead, if the timeline is short, you can focus better and get it done!

F. Follow the 80-20 rule mercilessly

The "80-20" rule says:

20% of your work will give you 80% results.

20% of the product features will be used 80% of the time.

20% of your customers will give you 80% of revenue and profits.

Prioritise the most important tasks by following the 80-20 rule. Learn to say "No". It will free up time to work on the 20% items that matter!

G. Avoid working from "home"

A common water cooler joke at corporate offices is when somebody is working "from home", he or she is working "for home".

Avoid working from home or rather, for home. If you don't have an office, mark a part of your home as your workspace. Treat it as your office, and work from there, just as you would do in a normal job.

While working from your "home office", pay attention to your attire. Dress exactly the way you would, if you were going out to work. Create a dress code for your company and follow it from Day One.

H. Be disciplined

Practice discipline. Be strict about deadlines. Take small steps. Win daily, even if it means winning small.

Self-discipline can be hard. There are too many distractions. Force yourself to learn it. It will help you take the best shot at success.

I. Learn to delegate

You will soon realise that you can't do everything on your own. You don't have the time and the skills. Start delegating. Empower your team. It will make them happy, it will make you happy. And most importantly, you will not be the bottleneck in making progress.

And finally,

J. Measure progress

When building a startup, it is very easy to feel direction-less. Nothing "great" might happen for a long time. How do you even know you are making progress every day? How do you know you are moving in the right direction?

Sangeet (Platformation Labs) created his own metrics to measure progress and to help him measure adoption, influence, and scalability of monetisation. He believes:

"From our childhood, we are used to a system. Whether it is school, college or job, there is an 'external control'. When you start something from scratch, there is no external control. You have to learn how to measure yourself, how to differentiate between progress and movement."

Create your own metrics of success and track them

religiously. Break down the metrics into smaller chunks, which you can track on a weekly, or even on a daily basis.

The objective is to keep you going, keep the team morale high, and to stay focused on doing the right things.

2. Team

Hiring is the #1 problem for most startups.

You compete with well-funded startups, high paying banking jobs, high flying consulting jobs, and secure corporate jobs.

You don't have a brand name to sell. You don't have enough cash to pay. You don't want to dilute your equity too much.

Manoj Kumar is an experienced recruitment specialist focused on startups in India (Kumar, 2016). He sums up the challenge on startup recruiting.

"On the recruiter side, there are few people who are willing to work with startups. Candidates look for stable jobs with good cash salary. Startups are seen as risky, offering less cash and more equity/ESOPs. Candidates don't understand the value of equity/ESOPs. Finally, candidates realise that they will have to work more in startups than regular jobs."

Almost all the founders who I spoke with faced challenges with recruiting. Many of them had to rely on their personal networks to find suitable talent.

Siddhartha Agrawal (Wallsoft Labs) says,

"One of the early challenges we faced was hiring the right development guys while ensuring that our trading platform's IP was not compromised. In fact, we waited for close to a year before making our first hiring, which happened in the form of a friend and colleague from our days at Microsoft."

Suhani Mohan (Saral Designs) says,

"Finding the right team, with no product and no money, was the most difficult task. Our friends would informally help us with a few activities like research on raw material suppliers and field visits. The first two people to join our team were also recommended by people in our network."

Brij Bhushan (Magicpin) sums it up:

"The hardest part was recruiting engineers. World class tech resources in India are not easy to hire for an early stage startup due to high salaries being offered and just generally paucity of genuinely high quality talent.

We were fortunate that we had a good network of well-wishers who recommended people.

We also ensured that we never let the lack of people came in the way of progress. We coded ourselves and used open source tools to maintain our momentum. It is easier to convince people to join a moving ship than a stationary one!"

Here are some thoughts around the decisions you will make on recruiting for your startup.

A. What skills to hire for?

Hire selectively for the most critical positions. In early days, only two positions are critical: Building the product or selling. Once you start scaling up, you can hire for other positions such as HR, finance, accounting, legal, and marketing.

B. Quality vs. Speed

In an ideal scenario, you want to hire people with the best skills, best track record, and best attitude for your startup. But such candidates are either expensive and/or unwilling to join you.

If you stick to a high-quality bar, you might not be able to hire anyone, or it may take too long to find someone. If you don't hire people, you lose precious time in building your product, in finding your customers, and proving your business model.

What do you do?

You make a trade-off. Time is your most precious asset and you can't afford to waste it.

If you don't get the best quality talent, do not stop. Hire. Be ready to make mistakes. Be ready to cover for bad hires. Be ready to fire bad hires before it is too late.

Sometimes, hiring is like dating. You can't wait forever. You have to make some compromises, some mistakes; you learn and you evolve. But you keep making progress.

C. Skill vs. Attitude

Manoj Kumar (Kumar, 2016) thinks startups are partially to blame for the challenges in hiring. He shares,

"Startups look for an ideal candidate—who is a 100% fit to the role with the right aptitude. Founders prefer aptitude more than attitude. They expect candidates to be like them."

If you can't find the best talent, look for people with a good attitude and previous experience in a startup environment.

People with the right attitude to learn can be a long-term asset for your company. Look for a willingness to learn, flexibility, comfort with ambiguity, and a desire to work hard. You can train them over time.

Past experience in a startup also helps. A startup environment can be very different from a regular corporate environment. Working hours are longer, roles are less clearly defined, financial incentives are often vague, career paths are unclear, there might be no well-defined HR policy, and the list goes on. If a person has worked in a similar environment, she will not expect corporate treatment when she joins your startup.

D. Part Time vs. Full Time

You might be tempted to hire "part-time" people. Don't.

Building a startup is a mission. You need 100% from your employees. You need full commitment and energy. Your startup must be the first and the only priority of each and every member on the team, and this can only happen when you hire full time resources.

Invest in retaining talent

The startup world is highly dynamic. People are impatient. People switch companies like they change clothes. Startups compete with each other and try to "steal" good employees by offering a better package.

Consider this scenario. You hire someone: let's call him Prem.

Month 1: Prem joins your company. You train him for a week, and then start allocating some real work.

Month 2: He ramps up, starts to become productive.

Month 5: You see full productivity. You are happy and start relying on Prem extensively.

Month 6: Prem tells you he has an offer in another company with a 40% salary increase. You have two options: Let him go and lose the momentum you've built up so far; or match the offer. Neither choice is ideal!

Retaining your best employees can be a challenge for other reasons too. Manoj (Kumar, 2016) highlighted typical reasons why employees leave startups.

1. False commitments by founders at the time of hiring
2. Lack of challenging work or unclear jobs
3. No defined growth path
4. Founders not showing confidence on employees

You can avoid these pitfalls.

How do you increase the chances of retaining your best team members?

First, design challenging roles

This one might surprise you. Wouldn't any role in a startup be challenging by default?

Not always. Many founders have a tendency to hold back the most interesting, the most critical, and the most challenging work for themselves. What is left might not be good enough for your employees.

As a founder, you have to learn to delegate to your team, or you run the risk of not only demotivating your team, but also becoming a bottleneck and a single point of failure for the startup.

Second, understand what motivates each individual on your team

A person joining a startup is different from others. Most likely she has compromised on financial cash incentives and is looking for something else. Understand what it is.

It might be recognition, the feeling of building something new, creating a team, or working on a cool problem. Understand what motivates your employees (beyond money) and find a way to provide it to them.

E. Create a good company culture

Culture is the glue of any team, of any company. As you think about culture, consider the two most important foundational elements: trust and communication.

In an earlier chapter, I talked about the importance of founders trusting each other. This applies to employees too. In a small, tightly knit setting of a startup, trust is critical. They must trust and support one other in this difficult journey. The moment trust breaks down, the startup is doomed for failure.

Trust starts with you. You have to trust your employees. Have confidence in them and delegate responsibilities and ownership. Do not treat them as "resources". The more you involve them in building your company, the more empowered they will feel, and the more productive they will be.

In return, your employees have to trust you. Fulfil your commitments towards them. Don't make false promises.

Learn to be a good communicator. Learn to share and be transparent. Share the progress of the startup with your employees regularly. Share the good and the bad. Don't keep them in the dark. The more you communicate, the more they will trust you.

3. Product/Service

In an earlier chapter, I highlighted the importance of setting up "controllable" milestones. For your product or service, you must add "Delivering a Minimum Viable Product (MVP) as a critical milestone. A MVP is a product which you can show to your customers and ask for money. Once you create your MVP, keep the following in mind:

A. Do not lose focus on Sales

Sales is an extremely critical element of a startup.

Are you already frowning at me? I understand!

Many of you, like me, are engineers. Often engineers under-estimate the importance of sales. We believe salesmen are frauds. "What is so difficult in selling my cool product?" "It will sell on its own" . . .and so on, we go, in our ignorant and incorrect thoughts.

As Peter Thiel, technology entrepreneur and investor says, "Sales matters as much as product."

As you are building your product iteratively, figure out how you will sell the product, as well as how will you reach your customer. Start selling. Test your selling process, in parallel with product. Tightly couple your product development to the sales process.

As a founder, you should know the sales process inside out. Keep yourself up-to-date on pipeline of customer opportunities and on various conversion metrics. Keep experimenting with different channels to reach out to customers. Know your customers and potential ones personally.

B. Be prepared to pivot

Once you create your MVP and launch it to potential customers, start gathering feedback about what they like or dislike in the product. Keep iterating on your product as you learn more about customer needs and preferences.

Do not be afraid to make course corrections if your original hypotheses prove to be incorrect, or if your business model is not working as expected.

Sabeer Bhatia and Jack Smith originally started building JavaSoft, a web-based personal directory system. While they were working on it, they realised a web-based email is a bigger idea. Hotmail was born (Livingston, 2007).

Evan Williams, the founder of two successful startups—Blogger.com and Twitter—first launched Pyra. Pyra was a web-based project management or collaboration tool. While building Pyra, he built a simple script to publish his thoughts in an easy way. He took the script, put it up on an internal site, and started using it to publish blogs for Pyra. This simple idea was later launched as Blogger.com (Livingston, 2007).

Flickr did not start as a full-fledged independent product. It was a small feature within the Game Neverending, being built by the founders. The founding team was focused on making the Game successful. But they saw an interesting thing: Flickr was taking off. Finally, they decided to stop developing the game and focus on building Flickr (Livingston, 2007).

Be agile in your product approach and be prepared to "pivot" if needed.

4. Cash

Pay attention to your startup's cash flow management. Even if you are profitable, you may not have any real cash to pay the bills if you are not smart about how cash flows into and out of your business. Learn basic accounting if you are running a company.

Here are some tips to avoid any surprises in handling your company's cash.

A. Draw a Minimum Survival Salary

If you are a co-founder or a CEO, set an example by withdrawing what I call Minimum Survival Salary.

The CEO of Box, a cloud storage and file sharing company, Aaron Levie, withdrew $150,000 as his salary, even after the company raised funds. For Silicon Valley, $150,000 is at best, an okay salary, and way lower than typical salaries.

If you are motivated by money, you will be tempted to draw a higher salary. However, it creates an unfavourable situation.

First reason is cash is the fuel for a startup. Any available cash should ideally be targeted towards driving growth in the startup. If you withdraw too much upfront, you leave little to re-invest in the company.

Second, as a founder, you not only have the highest risk, but also high reward (equity) in the event your startup succeeds. Claiming a high salary can result in a situation when you start enjoying the "status quo" with a good salary–not a good situation for your startup.

B. Be frugal

Once you start up, think twice about spending each penny of your startup money. Find creative ways to minimise expenses to save cash.

Here are some tips to manage your startup cash prudently.

C. Collect cash early

Push for favourable payment terms with your customers; try to get them to pay upfront. This can help tremendously with cash flow management.

D. Do not splurge

Don't buy a Ferrari when you can get away with a Maruti. Don't buy a Maruti, if you can get away with cabs. Don't cab it if you can use public transport.

Travel in economy class and book tickets well in advance for the best pricing. Stay in budget hotels.

No need for office space in expensive locations, expensive furniture, or expensive equipment.

Avoid unnecessary pizza parties, picnics, and eating at upscale restaurants. Each small expense adds up.

E. Avoid buying things, in general

Rent whenever possible. Do not buy furniture or office space, or even laptops and phones.

Do not buy servers; instead, buy variable capacity on the public cloud.

F. Get creative to find cheaper alternatives

Do you need that expensive PR firm? Can you use social marketing, instead of investing in banner ads? Can you use LinkedIn to create your pipeline, instead of hiring a new salesperson?

G. Spend where it matters

While keeping in mind all of the above, do spend on the right things, such as appreciating your employees, creating good working conditions, delighting customers, improving your product, building company culture, and on your mission.

H. Negotiate hard. Don't leave cash on the table

As an entrepreneur, you have to strengthen your negotiation skills. It is not an easy skill to learn, but master it, and you will reap long-term benefits.

In order to negotiate well, it is important to know the rules of the game.

Learn the rules of your industry. How are deals made? What are the typical terms and conditions? What are the margins? What is the typical revenue share split? What are the typical payment terms? The more you know about the industry, the better you will do in negotiations.

5. Self

It is important to take good care of yourself. You can't afford to lose "yourself." "**You**" are the most important asset of your startup.

Here are some tips to help you stay sane on this crazy journey.

A. Learn to be lonely

Sangeet (Platformation Labs) advises:

"Learn to be lonely. Even your team won't have the same level of passion and commitment as you."

Your startup journey is about you, it is about your dreams, it is about your ambition, and it is about your vision. At some point, you will have to battle it out alone. "*Ekla chaalo re*." Be prepared to fight out your struggles on your own even when no one else joins your path.

B. Expect the unexpected

Remember the age-old saying, "Nothing ever lasts—good and bad times."? It applies to startups too.

A startup journey can feel like a roller coaster ride. There will be ups and downs. Expect to be surprised.

Siddhartha Agrawal (Wallsoft Labs) says:

"Life as an entrepreneur throws a lot of unexpected challenges. There are fewer moments of comfort than more, because growing the company means facing problems that one had never thought or even known about."

Mohan Rajagopalan (Yaap.io) sums it up pretty well:

"You can't prepare for everything—so, enjoy the ride. When you are starting up, if you have one good day in a week, you are doing well. Over time it has been a process of increasing the good days and predicting the bad days."

C. Do not be afraid to make hard decisions

In his book *"The Hard Things about Hard Things"*, Ben Horowitz makes a profound statement.

"People always ask me, "What's the secret to being a successful CEO?" Sadly, there is no secret, but if there is one skill that stands out, it's the ability to focus and make the best move when there are no good moves. It's the moments where you feel most like hiding or dying that you can make the biggest difference as a CEO."

His book explains the challenges you will face as a CEO, the hard choices you will encounter, and how to think about deciding one way or the other. It is a must-read to prepare for life after you start up.

As a CEO, you will have to make many "do or die" decisions. Should you implement a new feature in your product? Should you raise funding? Should you accept a deal which can generate cash now, but may not be profitable in the longer term? Should you hire that person? Should you fire an employee? Should you tell your co-founder that he needs to step up?

Each one of these is a tough decision to make. Most of the time, there are no clear answers. Sometimes, the choices themselves may not be clear. But you have to take a call.

Srikrishnan Ganesan (Konotor) shares about his journey:

"It was definitely more stressful than I thought it would be. Having lead a team and having made many key decisions at a startup before, I had not imagined that being a founder would mean significantly more hard decisions and scenarios to deal with.

Making decisions on what's best for the company when you have employees and potential investors you are engaging is even harder—what's right for the team, what's right for the business, what's right for all stakeholders—you have to take a call and then see how it plays out for everyone."

I suggest three things to facilitate your decision-making process.

First, **be fact-based** as far as possible. Collect all facts and data. The more data based you are the less subjective and emotional you will be. Granted that not all the data you need might be available, but do try. Avoid decisions driven by emotions and bias.

Second, **use your "Why" as the guiding principle**. When you evaluate two choices, always remember why you decided on a startup in the first place. Be consistent with your "Why"; or you will lose track in your pursuit.

Let's take an example. Your mission is to solve a problem. Your product is not fully ready. But one day, you receive an offer giving you immediate cash. The offer will require you to significantly change your product—almost morph it into a completely new domain. What will you do? Will you stop your mission, and choose cash? Or will you stick to your mission and reject this deal?

Sangeet (Platformation Labs) faced two choice points; and his "Why" helped him make decisions.

"My first dilemma was 'push vs. pull'. Should I 'push' my ideas, or create 'pull'? Pushing is easier and shows immediate results but is not scalable. Pull is a long term game, but with immense scalability, once you hit a critical mass of adoption. There was always a temptation to push, and I had to force myself to think about creating pull. I'm glad I did this, today there's global adoption for my work that could only be achieved through best case scenario of pull.

My second dilemma was 'influence vs. money'. Do I monetise immediately, or create a sustainable influence? Again, this is a choice between short term and long term. I focused on creating influence. This helped me scale my monetisation rapidly. If I had prioritised monetisation over influence, I would never have been able to scale it.

Stick to your "Why". You will face many dilemmas and choice points. You will face distractions. Revert back to 'Why' you are doing all this."

Finally, **once you have made the choice, be comfortable with the outcome**. As a philosopher once said, "It is not difficult to make a choice. It is difficult to live with it."

You will be right and wrong. Of course, you would hope

you are more right than wrong. But you won't be right 100% of the time. Be comfortable with making poor decisions. In hindsight, you can change many things. But you don't have the benefit of hindsight when you are making the decision. It is okay to make mistakes. Learn from them and move on.

D. Stay connected with friends and family

Coca Cola's former CEO Bryan Dyson made a famous speech, in which he talks about five balls of life (shinecoachingbarcelona. com/en/5-balls-of-life-brian-dyson-speech/). He said,

"Imagine life as a game in which you are juggling some five balls in the air. You name them work, family, health, friends and spirit. And you're keeping all of these in the air. You will soon understand that work is a rubber ball. If you drop it, it will bounce back. But the other four balls—family, health, friends, and spirit—are made of glass. If you drop one of these, they will be irrevocably scuffed, marked, nicked, damaged or even shattered. They will never be the same. You must understand that and strive for balance in your life."

Sometimes, the fear of difficult startup related conversations with concerned family members and friends can make you want to isolate yourself. Other times, even if you want to stay in touch, it gets pushed to the bottom of your to-do list.

Whatever be the case, it is important to realise that starting up can be an incredibly lonely experience and you need all the support you can get.

Make time several times a week, if not daily, to connect with your close family members—whether through a quick phone call, email or face to face visit. Meet local friends over coffee (or have a meal together!) and schedule periodic hangouts with distant ones. Send a Diwali/Christmas/New Year greeting to remind those who matter, that you have not forgotten them.

Feeling connected and loved can help keep you motivated and energised, and staying in touch is not necessarily the chore it is made out to be.

E. Maintain and build your professional network

Maintain your connection with your current world. Your current manager, colleagues, and partners might help you get back, if and when you need to get back. They can also help keep in touch with the latest developments, and possibly become your supporters and (in the best case) customers of your startup product/service.

Join a meetup or attend a startup networking event; it can put you in touch with others just like you with whom you can exchange ideas and feedback.

F. Build your personal brand – share your experience on social media

Launching a startup is a unique and enriching experience. You grow as a professional and as a person. You are catapulted into so many different and difficult situations—with every situation presenting a learning opportunity.

Suhani Mohan (Saral Designs) found startup life to be a great learning experience.

"I have learnt so much more about so many more tangible and intangible things in the last two years than I ever learnt in my entire academic + work life together."

As an entrepreneur, you can leverage these experiences and learnings to define your personal brand.

One of the ways to do it is document your experiences on social media. I recommend using LinkedIn Blogs to publish your startup experiences regularly. Share what you are learning, what you are going through. Paint your journey. Share your triumphs and struggles.

It can help in multiple ways. It can communicate your story to the world. It can help others understand what you are doing, what you are learning, what you are creating, and the impact of this journey on you. As a bonus, it can help you connect with other budding and veteran entrepreneurs, who will in turn, share their own viewpoints.

Tactically, it helps keep you in front of your network. People are busy, and then tend to forget. If you document your story well, they will know what you are up to. If and when the time comes, it will pave the way to reach out to your supporters and you won't find it difficult to ask for help.

And finally,

G. Take care of your health

Starting up can get incredibly busy and your health can take a backseat.

Don't make that mistake. Health is wealth. There is no point in being successful or building piles of money, if you are not around to enjoy it.

Exercise, eat right, and take time to rest and recharge.

In Closing,

My dear Reader, my simple premise throughout this book has been that preparation helps you lower your risks. This premise is applicable not only to the "Before you start" phase, but also "After you start". Once you start working on building a business, you have to constantly look out for ways to reduce your risk and come up trumps.

Remember:

The more you prepare, the more you know.

The more you know, the less surprised you are.

The less surprised you are, the better equipped you will be.

The more equipped you are, the lower the risk you will face.

I hope you have enjoyed reading this book, and that it will help you in your journey to start up.

Leave your thoughts/feedback/comments if any @pango on twitter. I will be delighted to hear from you!

BIBLIOGRAPHY

Interviews

Agrawal, S, Founder WallSoft. "How did you prepare for your startup?" Interview by P. Goyal. Published at https://howtopreparetostartup.wordpress.com, July, 2016.

Bhushan, B, Founder MagicPin. "How did you prepare for your startup?" Interview by P. Goyal. Published at https://howtopreparetostartup.wordpress.com, August, 2016.

Choudhary, A, Founder BlogVault. "How did you prepare for your startup?" Interview by P. Goyal. Published at https://howtopreparetostartup.wordpress.com, August, 2016.

Choudhary, S P, Founder Platformation Labs. "How did you prepare for your startup?" Interview by P. Goyal. Published at https://howtopreparetostartup.wordpress.com, September, 2016.

Khandelwal, N, Founder QuantInsti. "How did you prepare for your startup?" Interview by P. Goyal.

Published at https://howtopreparetostartup.wordpress.com, October, 2016.

Gandhi, K, Founder LogicRoots. "How did you prepare for your startup?" Interview by P. Goyal. Published at https://howtopreparetostartup.wordpress.com, June, 2016.

Ganesan, S., Founder Konotor (acquired by Freshdesk). "How did you prepare for your startup?" Interview by P. Goyal. Published at https://howtopreparetostartup.wordpress.com, October, 2016.

Jadhav, C., Founder VirtualMob. "How did you prepare for your startup?" Interview by P. Goyal. Published at https://howtopreparetostartup.wordpress.com, October, 2016.

Kumar, M., Startup recruitment specialist. "What are the challenges faced by startups in hiring?" Interview by P. Goyal. Published at https://howtopreparetostartup.wordpress.com, October, 2016.

Mohan, S, Founder Saral Designs. "How did you prepare for your startup?" Interview by P. Goyal. Published at https://howtopreparetostartup.wordpress.com, July, 2016.

Rajagoplan, M., Founder Yaap.io. "How did you prepare for your startup?" Interview by P. Goyal. Published at https://howtopreparetostartup.wordpress.com, July, 2016.

Sachan, M., Founder LendingKart. "How did you prepare for your startup?" Interview by P. Goyal. Published at https://howtopreparetostartup.wordpress.com, October, 2016.

Sankhla, D., Founder Alohomara Foundation. "How did you prepare for your startup?" Interview by P. Goyal. Published at https://howtopreparetostartup.wordpress.com, October, 2016.

BOOKS

Grant, A. *"Originals: How Non-Conformists Move the World."* Penguin Books, 2017.

Ferriss, T. *"The 4-Hour WorkWeek."* Potter/TenSpeed/Harmony, 2009.

Thiel, P. *"Zero to One."* Crown Publishing Group, 2014.

Sinek, S. *"Start with Why: How Great Leaders Inspire Everyone to Take Action."* Portfolio; Reprint edition, 2011.

Reiss, E. *"The Lean Startup."* Crown Business, 2011.

Murphy, B. *"The Intelligent Entrepreneur: How Three Harvard Business School Graduates Learned the 10 Rules of Successful Entrepreneurship."* St. Martin's Griffin, 2011.

Livingston, J. *"Founders at Work: Stories of Startups' Early Days."* APress, 2007.

Horowitz, B. *"The Hard Thing About Hard Things."* HarperBusiness, 2014.

RESEARCH PUBLICATIONS

Joseph Raffiee, J. F. "Why Going All-In on Your Start-Up Might Not Be the Best Idea." Harvard Business Review, 2014

Kanter, R. M. (n.d.). "Mark Zuckerberg and Misery as Motivation."

Noam Wasserman, T. H. "The Very First Mistake Most Startup Founders Make." Harvard Business Review, February 23, 2016

APPENDIX

(Figures and tables)

Pankaj Goyal grew up in a typical Indian middle class family in Jaipur, India. In a family of government employees, he followed the standard script to build a career: "Work hard on academics and get the highest scores." After getting his Bachelors in Computer Science from IIT Kanpur and an MBA from IIM Bangalore, Pankaj landed a dream job with McKinsey & Company, the leading management consulting firm. He started working in the Brussels, Belgium office. But he always had an itch. . . an itch to start a company. He left the consulting job after a year and landed in New Delhi to start up in 2008.

Pankaj's startup experience was bitter-sweet. The business saw early success and generated good cash, but failed to grow. He ran it for three years and decided to quit.

In 2011, he got married and moved to the USA. Ever since, he has continued to work in his area of passion: technology. These days he is focused on applying Artificial Intelligence to solve the toughest problems being faced by businesses. He continues to be involved in the world of entrepreneurship as an angel investor and as an advisor to startups in the Silicon Valley and India.